$1-

D0001011

WALLABY

Other titles
by Steve Strandemo with Bill Bruns:

The Racquetball Book

ADVANCED RACQUETBALL

by
Steve Strandemo
with
Bill Bruns

Photographs by Jack Miller

WALLABY

A Wallaby Book
Published by Simon & Schuster
New York

Copyright © 1981 by Steve Strandemo and Bill Bruns

All rights reserved
including the right of reproduction
in whole or in part in any form
Published by Wallaby Books
A Simon & Schuster Division of Gulf & Western Corporation
Simon & Schuster Building
Rockefeller Center
1230 Avenue of the Americas
New York, New York 10020

WALLABY and colophon are registered trademarks of Simon & Schuster

Designed by Leonard Telesca

First Wallaby Books printing November 1981

Manufactured in the United States of America

Printed and bound by The Murray Printing Company.

10 9 8 7 6 5
ISBN 0-671-79150-8

To my writer, Bill Bruns, whose writing excellence and organization made this book special; to Jack Miller, whose illustrative photography made this book easy to understand; and to my wife, Terry, whose patience and guidance made *Advanced Racquetball* a reality.

Steve Strandemo
San Diego, California

I dedicate this book to my father whom I will always remember for his wisdom, his guidance, his enthusiasm, and the sincerity of his friendship. My life has been enriched because I knew him and I am thankful that our paths crossed for so many good years. Both my mother and I will miss him very much.

CONTENTS

CHAPTER 1

THE FUNDAMENTALS OF ADVANCED PLAY

Racquetball has been described as a sport in which "any semblance of stroking style is probably accidental" and where "98 percent of the strategy is based on hitting the ball as hard as you can." This may certainly be true for beginners, and even for those players who can intimidate opponents with their uncontrolled power. However, if you're hooked on this game as a competitive outlet, I'm sure that an important motivation is the endlessly absorbing challenge it presents for you to play well and to reach higher skill levels. Advanced racquetball, played the way it is intended, is not a mindless, helter-skelter, let-it-rip contest where neither player knows where the next shot may end up. It's a game of power, but also of patience and control, and many pieces must all fit together—reliable strokes, intelligent shot selection, efficient court coverage, and a grasp of match-play tactics.

My presumption is that you're familiar with the basic shots and strategy, and you have a playing style that is comfortable for you—but you're looking for ways to play better under pressure and to win more matches, whether among your regular playing partners, opponents on the challenge ladder at your club, or in league and tournament competition. If you're willing to experiment with concepts and techniques that may challenge you to change the way you play now, then I'm confident I can help you make important breakthroughs to better play. There are creative ways to gain a better mastery of this game, and I'll give you practical, realistic guidelines that have been gleaned from three perspectives: (1) my own experience as a playing pro since 1973, (2) my teaching experience giving summer camps and clinics around the country, and (3) my own homework—watching numerous amateur tournaments and substantiating my judgments through videotape analysis and matches at every playing level. So I know how the game *should* be played, but I'm also familiar with the common problems that might be limiting your efficiency as you play—and your progress.

To lay the groundwork for the rest of the book, this first chapter will describe the crucial concepts underlying advanced play, whether you're a C player in San Diego or an open player in Wisconsin. This overall approach I'm presenting is reality—the way the top pros strive to play the game today after years of emulating one another, experimenting with new theories, and continually refining their games as they've searched for those methods of hitting the ball and covering the court that work best for them, with prize money and rankings at stake. There isn't a mystery style you must uncover as you try to work your way up to the next playing level. What counts is how well you can execute the key fundamentals while adding the important nuances through experience and common sense.

TEN CRUCIAL CHECKPOINTS

Racquetball is still a young sport, several hundred how-to books behind golf and tennis. Yet while stroking techniques and tactical philosophies are continuing to evolve, only so much evolution can take place inside this 20-by-40-foot court we play on. And now that the game has been sufficiently influenced by two distinct playing styles—control and power—we can isolate the most important elements and blend them together into "advanced racquetball." Check your own game against the following list of characteristics the top players share in their overall playing style. You may come in at the struggling end of a particular fundamental, or you may have already successfully incorporated it into your game. But whatever your playing level, I hope this list will challenge you and open your eyes to ways you can advance your playing ability by developing a well-rounded game. When you go to work on your game, periodically review these guidelines to see specific areas in which you have improved . . . and where work still remains.

1. On both forehands and backhands, you have the stroking techniques—and an *aggressive* attitude—that when an offensive opportunity exists, you try to either kill the ball, angle it away from your mispositioned opponent, or at least hit it low enough so that it takes its second bounce before caroming off the back wall. This gives you offensive weapons that keep constant pressure on your opponents.

2. You have good solid swings on the forehand and backhand that enable you to minimize your exploitable areas, allowing you to hit with strong force and accuracy—into your offensive "low zone" and to the ceiling—so that you're not at the mercy of an opponent who can direct the ball into the back corners or tight along the side walls and score at will.

3. When serving, you have the correct mechanics (for instance, a two-step motion into the ball) and you know your front-wall targets so that you can drive your opponents deep into the back corners with properly placed low drives and hard "Z's," while minimizing the setups that come off the side and back walls. You also mix in correctly

angled half-lobs and high-lobs that keep your opponent on the defensive.

4. After serving, you relocate quickly and efficiently behind the service box as you study your opponent to see if he's going for an offensive return or if he's going to the ceiling—and you're ready to react accordingly.

5. When returning a serve, you are able to react and move quickly to either corner and you have the strokes to hit effective offensive returns or, if the serve is really tough, to go defensively to the ceiling.

6. You cover the back half of the court (the "action zone") with a blend of quickness, strength, and agility—plus an attitude that you want to try to put the ball away at every appropriate opportunity. In the front part of this area (center court) you know when to cut the ball off and when to let it come off the back wall. In the deeper part, during low-zone rallies, ceiling ball exchanges, and against the serve, you use common sense in deciding when to be offensive and when to go back up to the ceiling.

7. You have good "adaptable" form from varying stances so that you can hit quickly and forcefully, with a good degree of accuracy, when you don't have time to take your normal swing or you're not in a position to step into the ball (for example, in center-court or when the ball is driven by you and you must stretch and reach to make the hit).

8. Going into an important match, you've thought about a "game plan" and an alternate strategy, you're warmed up properly, and you're ready to play at full throttle on the very first point.

9. You can adjust your game to the type of ball being used, your opponent's particular playing style, and the patterns of a rally and the match. When you're ahead you stick with what's working; when you're behind you make strategy changes and use time-outs to gain the momentum back.

10. Percentage racquetball is your goal: you know the

value of power *and* control and you strive to blend both elements; you have a sense of when to hit the ball offensively and when to go to the ceiling; you strive for a put-away but you minimize skips; you maneuver your opponent around the court with solid shots—passes, pinches, straight-in and cross-court kill attempts, and ceiling balls; and you recognize the importance of using one shot to set up an easier second shot, rather than having an all-or-nothing philosophy of shot-making.

THE 20-by-20 CONCEPT

While researching this book, I charted tournament matches at every level of play, looking for statistical patterns, and I was amazed by one basic similarity: after the serve and service return, over 80 percent of the shots in a match—and often 90 percent—are taken from behind the service box. Agreed, this is a game of kill-shot attempts, but only rarely do we have time to actually move into the service box or closer to dig up those shots; the ball either dies in front of us or comes into the back half of the court. In other words, *this game is played deeper—far more often—than we commonly think*, and this dictates several basic premises for advanced play.

First, although the court is 40 feet long and 20 feet wide, your success is actually going to depend upon how effectively you learn to cover the entire back 20-by-20 area—what I term the "action zone." Eventually you're going to need the ability to thrust forward to dig up shots in the service box, but day in and day out you'll prove yourself in the back 20-by-20 area as you cover and hit groundstrokes, volleys, ceiling balls, and other shots.

Second, to maximize your efficiency inside the action zone—in terms of both coverage and shot-making—you may find that you need to cover your opponent's offensive shots from a slightly deeper position than you may be presently playing. Your basic coverage position should fluctuate from around 23 feet to 28 or 29 feet, depending upon your opponent's position and his ability to put away the shot you've given him.

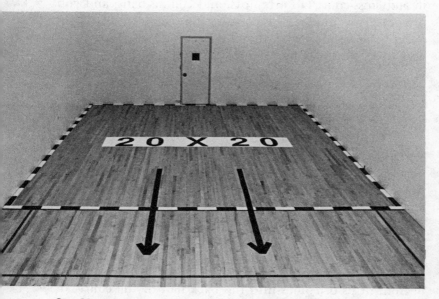

Over 80 to 90 percent of the shots in a rally are taken from the 20-by-20-foot area behind the service box. Advanced players are efficient at covering all parts of this "action zone" and, as the arrows indicate, have the ability to thrust and stretch forward into the service box to dig up potential kill shots.

Third, instead of worrying about being in a position to dig up your opponent's perfect winners in the front 15-foot area, be much more concerned about your readiness to cover the shots he leaves up, because nearly all of them will carry back to the action zone. Make that critical breakthrough by learning to cover your opponent's offensive shots with an attitude of "I'll concede you any shot that bounces twice inside of 15 feet—since this is basically an irretrievable area—and instead I'm going to play off all of your mistakes." It's true, of course, that as your playing level moves up, your opponents will be hitting an increasing number of successful kills. However, the problem isn't going to be your positioning, but the fact that you're probably giving them far too many offensive opportunities. Keep the pressure on with accurate shot-making and even your toughest opponent will continually leave the ball up, giving you a chance to score again.

If your progress has leveled off, one major factor holding you back may be that you're trying to buck reality by constantly rushing up near the back service line as your opponent goes to hit, thinking you can add some pressure and also dig up more kill attempts. True, you may make the occasional spectacular rekill from up here, but far more of your opponent's shots are going to come back into the action zone that jam you or easily angle past you. You put too much pressure on yourself while giving your opponent greater leeway in his shot selection.

The reason nearly all shots are taken in the back half of the court once the rally begins is that *the ball carries deeper than we tend to realize* (and much more frequently). This is a game where inches on the front wall dictate feet on the court, and the slightest error in accuracy is magnified, especially when there's good pace on the ball. For example, if a skilled player varies his shots more than 12 inches up and down on the front wall and maintains the same velocity, it means the difference between a successful kill shot and a setup off the back wall. Even a straight-in kill attempt that hits just 12 inches high will actually take its *first* bounce near the front red line (15 feet) and then carry well into the action zone. (If you're not convinced, get on a court and just drive balls hard into the front wall from about 25 to 30 feet and watch where they take their first bounce and the second bounce—in relation to how high they were hit. It helps to have a friend stand near the front wall and mark the spot where each shot hits. Look for the same relationships the next time you watch a match.)

Even a kill attempt that hits just 12 inches high on the front wall will usually take its first bounce near the front red line and its second bounce about 25 to 30 feet from the front wall—in the opponent's prime hittable range.

The Virtues of a Deeper Coverage Position

When you fluctuate your prime coverage position from about 23 feet back to almost 30 feet, here are the advantages you gain over a more inflexible position just behind the service box:

● You'll feel more in control of your play because you'll be getting jammed less often.

● You'll be much less vulnerable to having the ball driven constantly by you, cross-court or down-the-line.

● With slightly more time to react to the ball, you'll reach more shots. That extra split second can also make the difference between setting up on a shot or just flicking the ball back to the front wall.

● You gain much greater efficiency in the action zone; you can cover a bigger area more effectively because you're more equidistant from the shots that you'll be forced to hit.

Perhaps you're wondering, "If I lag deeper against a hard hitter in my different coverage positions, doesn't this simply give him more room to kill the ball in the front court?" Yes, but only slightly. Since his ball has added pace, his shots have greater depth and he must keep his kill attempts very low on the front wall to keep them from rebounding back to you in the action zone. Also, power players are far less accurate than you might think when they have to hit while on the move, stretched out, or when they don't have time to uncork on the ball. So lay back a bit and realize that you're putting pressure on the shooter to execute, for he knows that when he has the shot, he has to make it. If he errs to the high side, then you're ready to cover his shot when it comes into the action zone; you have slightly more time to get into position and this will help your execution, which in turn should lead to more winners for you.

Testing the 20-by-20 Concept

If you're still hesitant that you should maintain deeper coverage positions than you may use now, do some objective homework and find out for yourself why some changes in your approach to this game could be dictated.

First, chart matches between players at different ability levels. In the first game, put a dot on a court diagram to indicate where every shot is taken after the service return. In the second game, note how few kill-shots attempts actually die in the front 15 feet versus those that travel into the action zone.

Second, have a friend chart you and an opponent during the first game of a serious match, noting where both of you take all of your shots after the service return. In the second game, have your friend chart only your shots.

Third, get on a court and see for yourself just how low you must hit the front wall to make the ball bounce twice before the front red line (15 feet). Then, as you hit from about 30 feet, have your friend indicate where each shot hits the front wall while you watch to see where the second bounce occurs.

Fourth, when watching matches at your club, notice where players are positioning themselves as their opponent hits—and where the ball takes its second bounce.

Fifth, in practice matches try to analyze how often the ball is coming to you in the desired hitting zone—from calf to thigh height—and where you were positioned for that particular shot as your opponent went to hit.

(You may find that you only have to play a long stride deeper than you presently do, but a 2-to-4-foot change on a court this size can be tremendously important in adapting your game to basic realities and to the kind of racquetball you want to play. See Chapter 9 for a fuller discussion of court coverage.)

THE OVERALL GOAL: POWER WITH CONTROL

Your ability to hit with power is crucial in today's game—and can help move you many pegs up the ladder—but aimless, uncontrolled power will get you in as much trouble as the good that it brings and will sabotage your efforts to develop a sound game. Conversely, you can't expect to win big matches with a totally defensive game, where you simply keep the ball in play by hitting ceiling balls, passing shots, and lob serves while waiting for your opponent to make all the errors.

Ideally, the goal to strive for is what we might call "controlled maximum velocity," where you blend power and control in your strokes, your shot selection, and your overall approach to the game. The realists in advanced racquetball are learning that to become complete players who can adjust to every type of opponent, they must develop confidence in their ability to play with both power and control.

Keeping Power in Perspective

The great virtue of controllable power is that it enables you to play tough against any type of player. When you can pound the ball accurately, low enough to keep it from coming off the back wall as a setup, you generate more mistakes by your opponent (such as left-up shots and balls that carom unintended off a side wall) because you cut down on his reaction time and put him on the defensive—either by jamming him or forcing him to move quickly and to hit while on the move or stretched out. This lowers his scoring efficiency while increasing your offensive opportunities.

For example, power with control will nearly always beat the adept control player because you can hit at a speed that minimizes his chances to set up comfortably and hit accurately and thus keep the game controlled to his liking. This same power in your game will help keep the blaster at bay by keeping him under constant pressure. As one of the original control-era pros, I've had to change my swings on the forehand and backhand to gain more power. Now I can hit the ball hard enough to stay in the rally against the "shooters" and create my own offensive opportunities. Power itself is not the crucial factor when killing the ball straight-in or as a pinch—accuracy is what counts—but it does help give you more chances for the knockout punch by putting your opponent on the defensive and forcing weak returns.

Therefore, have an appreciation for power (and study Chapters 2 and 3 for ways to add it to your forehand and backhand), but remember *that your ability to sting the ball unbelievably hard is not enough to keep you advancing if you can't keep the ball low with a minimum of skips.* If you're a dedicated shooter and you're on your game and getting setups from your opponent, you'll bury him. But when you're out of the groove and wild, your opponent doesn't have to be awed or intimidated by your power—he must simply hang in there until you skip the ball or wait for his chance to rekill your shots in center-court, off a side wall, or off the back wall.

The Important Elements of Control

Increasingly, as I see the game evolving, a preoccupation with all-out power can't hide the fact that the big hitters must know how to hit good ceiling balls and passing shots as well as the control player.

First of all, whatever your playing style, there are many times in a match when you have no other logical choice but to go to the ceiling—in response to an opponent's well-placed serve, when you don't have a good offensive opportunity during the rally, and when his ceiling ball dictates another ceiling return. As much as fellow pro Marty Hogan may be identified as the ultimate blaster, he doesn't crunch every shot from all over the court; he flips to the ceiling when he can't be accurately offensive and he will stay in the ceiling rally with a nice feathery touch until his opponent makes an error or he gets a better shot.

Second, as you add power to your game, you'll find that you need help from your opponent—in terms of left-up shots—and perfect timing in order to build your attack around kill-shot attempts. Instead of trying to live-or-die with a power approach like this, master your down-the-line and cross-court passing angles so that you can also move the ball around the court and thus keep your opponents on the move. This realization came to a junior player from Illinois, who was working out in San Diego and who told me, "All of a sudden the guy standing next to me is hitting just as hard—or maybe harder—than I am, plus he's much more accurate. I've always depended on power to win all my matches, but now I realize I've got to get with some of the smarter pros and *learn how to play.*" What he needed was to incorporate power and control together.

PLAYING THE PERCENTAGES WITH A KILL-SHOT PHILOSOPHY

Many power players believe they've got to "hit the bottom boards" ultimately to play this game right. They like the spectacular approach, often getting into competition with other power players to see who can hit the most phenomenal kill shot with the most velocity. Yet since their margin of error is so small between a skip, a winner, and a setup off the back wall, they end up playing a "feast-or-famine" type of game. I certainly favor an aggressive, offensive approach to racquetball, but one that also takes reality into mind, and the percentages. Since you can't depend on the spectacular kill to win matches week in and week out, here's my shot-making philosophy in a capsule: *Go for winners at every reasonable opportunity, but* (1) minimize your skips, (2) try to keep the ball from coming off the back wall, and (3) learn to use good passing angles and pinches to create additional scoring opportunities.

Low
Zone

The Low-Zone Approach

Offensive efficiency begins with an understanding of your "low-zone" target areas, on the front and side walls. There's a two-stage process here, relative to your particular ability.

At first, as you are building a foundation for advanced shot-making, visualize your offensive target area as a 3-foot-

▲
In advanced play, your low-zone target area from virtually any place on the court will move lower on the front wall and extend back along both side walls—for kill attempts and effective passes and pinches.

◄ The hitter is aiming for her low-zone target area on the left half of the front wall, below about 3 feet. The lines on the court indicate her prime angles for straight-in and cross-court kills and passes.

high net stretching from the nearest side wall (including your pinch-shot angle) to midcourt on the front wall. By hitting into your low-zone area, you're aiming for a kill but your higher misses will still bounce twice on the floor before reaching the back wall (or will barely carry off the wall). This gives you good passing shots or low, hard drives into the heart of the action zone that puts constant pressure on your opponent. By focusing on that low zone as you go to hit, and executing an attitude that "I'm going for winners, but I must get the ball to bounce twice before the back wall," you're not giving your opponent setups and you maximize his potential for error. Against your passing shots, he must either try to cut the ball off or hustle deep, knowing that if it gets past him, you'll score on the shot.

Stage two comes gradually as your skill level rises and you hit with greater confidence into your low-zone area. You must break this monolithic block into specific target areas for pinches and passing shots and move them lower. The pros find they must constantly be hitting below 12 inches as they strive to observe the two-bounce maxim when they fail on their kill attempts. Keep thinking "low zone" as you play, but become more exact in hitting your targets, since your opponents will be more efficient at scoring off your 3-foot-high misses that come into the action zone.

Minimize Your Skip Shots

Ultimately, you should be constantly funneling in and saying, "I'm aiming low and I'm going for winners—but I don't want to skip the ball in." When you can play with this attitude and you're not giving your opponents gift points with constant skips, you force them to beat you with good shots and they must all deal with you. Certainly skips are going to happen as you gain more power and you're forced to hit the ball closer to the floor, but don't accept them as a natural trade-off for being offensive. If you're

If you fail to put the ball away for a kill, your next goal is to hit the ball low enough to make it bounce twice before coming off the back wall.

hitting more skips than winners, you're not playing with common sense; you're taking too much responsibility off your opponent and digging your own hole. Why gamble with a "bottom-board" philosophy, trying for perfect rollouts, when you can raise your aim a couple of inches and still hit winners? If you're going to error, learn to do so on the high side and force your opponent to reexecute a good shot. Also remember that many times your opponent will be out of position as you go to hit, and just good placement on your part—away from your opponent—will do the job as well as a flat-out kill.

Be Patient in Creating Scoring Opportunities

Advanced racquetball often turns into a flailing duel when two players go toe to toe, hitting the ball as hard as they can until the rally ends with some kind of a kill shot or a skip. You want to be able to rip with the hitters—when the opportunity is there—but I feel it's also crucial to know how to play a more patient game where you use well-executed passing shots and pinches to force the weak returns that give you safer kill attempts. (Chapter 7 will discuss ways you can hone the accuracy of your pinch shots and passes.)

WORKING ON HITTING THE BALL LOW

1.   Determine your general low-zone area by standing about 30 to 35 feet from the front wall and hitting the ball straight in, low and hard, until you learn how far up you can hit and still have the ball bounce twice on the floor before it hits the back wall.

2.   Mark off your low-zone area with a horizontal line and play a practice match with a friendly opponent, while a friend in the gallery charts how many of your offensive

shots hit below the line (as kills, skips, and others) and how many hit above (noting how many come off the back wall as setups). These statistics should help you be objective about your game, in terms of realizing just how few shots actually hit in the low zone and knowing the relative role played by skips and kills.

3. Use practice drills and practice matches to gain confidence at hitting the ball as low as you can without skipping the ball in. Developing the right mental approach is enhanced when you get into situations where you can attempt kill shots without being inhibited by the fear of losing the rally with a skip.

4. If you're going for your low-zone area, always try to be thinking "Shoot down," however high you're contacting the ball. There's a relentless attitude required here, a persistence to stay low with the ball as you play.

THE INFLUENCE OF THE BALL

We know that the type of ball being used (slow or fast) will influence how a match is played and perhaps force some slight adjustments in target areas. However, the smart players prepare for any eventuality by becoming familiar with all types of balls in practice sessions. They can then take any match as it comes, adjusting to however the ball might be affecting play. My feeling is that if you can develop sound strokes and a grasp on basic strategy, you can adapt the fundamentals in this book to any speed of ball and play a solid game of racquetball. For instance, if you're going to play in a tournament, find out in advance what make of ball will be used (which is usually noted on the entry blank) and then practice and play with that ball for a couple of weeks before the tournament.

CHAPTER 2

THE FOREHAND

Win or lose, most experienced racquetball players are pretty comfortable with their forehand stroke. It's their most frequent offensive weapon, the stroke they use when serving low drives and "Z's," and the stabilizing part of their game. "My forehand is reliable; I know where it's going," is what I commonly hear. Yet I also know that most players are looking for increased power—with control—as they strive to develop a more total game. So before you try to skip past this chapter, let's be objective. Just how effective is your forehand when you have a chance to set up? Can you consistently pound it into your low zone—as a straight-in kill, a pinch, or a passing shot—and keep your opponent on the move? Or does the ball constantly come back to him around the middle of the court, where he cuts it off or lets it come off the back wall? Is your forehand a scoring threat at 25 feet? At 30 feet? At 35 feet? Or does it simply keep the rally alive the farther back you're pushed? On reflection—and by having your own matches charted—do you find yourself hitting more skips than winners?

However your forehand checks out, this chapter can help you refine the stroke that you have as we work toward

an ultimate goal: a sound, repetitious swing that enables
you to hit with power and control all the way back to 38
feet, and that will come through for you under pressure.
*There's an overall racquetball swing that we can emulate,
with five or six fundamental elements that need to be
grooved within that swing.* Contrary to a common myth,
this is not a forgiving game at the advanced level if you
wildly miss your target areas against a smart opponent.
Agreed, your high misses will remain in play and can even
work to your benefit if the ball angles away from your opponent or comes directly into him, forcing a difficult "reflex" return. Yet basically you're simply prolonging the
agony with consistently inaccurate shots, for eventually an
efficient opponent is going to hit too many winners off your
setups.

Therefore, don't underestimate the importance of accurate stroking technique off both sides, forehand and backhand, in making everything you learn about shot-selection
tactics meaningful.

THE GRIP

Personally, I favor switching between conventional forehand and backhand grips as I move to the ball. Changing
grips now comes reflexively and I find that it facilitates a
more natural wrist-snapping motion in the contact zone
and a flat swing coming through the ball.

Two reminders if you're switching grips: (1) learn to
keep the racquet relatively loose in your hitting hand as
you make the change with your fingers, and (2) don't let
the opposite hand "help" out. Interference by the off-hand
can develop into a bad habit that limits your quickness in
setting up properly, especially during fast-action exchanges.
Try holding a ball in your nonhitting hand to help avoid or
break this habit when you're practicing.

If you've learned to hold one grip for all your strokes—in between the two conventional grips—stay with it, providing the racquet is comfortable in your hand as you swing and you make good solid contact. But if you're having trouble keeping the ball low, the likely culprit could be your grip; it will cause the racquet face to be tilted back slightly at impact—thus raising your shots—when you fail to make adjustments in your swing. Instead of making those adjustments, which demand greater timing in the contact zone, try to master two conventional grips. Practice changing grips, on and off the court, and eventually this will become a second-nature reaction when you see the ball coming.

KEY ELEMENTS OF THE SWING

Set Up Early and Quickly

The earlier you can take your racquet up to a solid set position on the backswing—with your hitting arm bent and

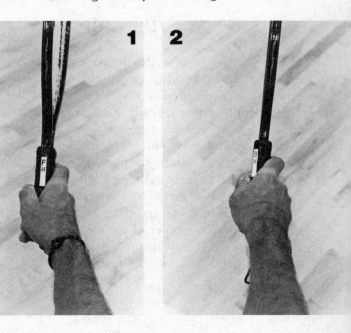

raised to around shoulder level—the easier it will be for you to groove a synched swing that utilizes the power in your body. The game will seem much less of a panic from shot to shot and you'll have more time to move down through the ball with good body action.

Even if you're confident that you're setting up early, have a friend watch your next match (or videotape part of one game) and look for two key checkpoints:

First, do you pull your racquet back and up quickly as the ball approaches? Or, are you waiting until the last possible moment, even when there's ample time to set up earlier? If you discover that you're late—a universal problem for aspiring advanced players—then the ball is always going to be on top of you, forcing you into a rushed, ineffective "punch" swing in order to get the racquet through in time. When you don't have time to use your entire body to generate power (and to absorb most of the load), you must compensate by swinging harder with your arm, and this constant trauma can lead to a throbbing elbow and a sore arm that grows weary in a tough match.

Second, is your non-hitting hand touching the racquet

THE BASIC GRIPS

This is the conventional forehand grip (1), with the "V" formed by the thumb and index finger lying on top of the racquet handle as you look down.

For the conventional backhand grip (2), the "V" shifts slightly to the left, directly on top of the left diagonal bevel on the racquet handle.

To hold one grip for both strokes (3), have the "V" lie between the conventional grips.

1 2

handle as you're switching grips or setting up? This is a common flaw—and an unnecessary movement—that can cause you to be late on your backswing, yet only videotaping with slow-motion may convince you that you're actually doing it.

A Higher Setup for More Power

An important development in forehand technique since my first book was published (in 1977) has been the evolution to a higher racquet setup, with power hitters now raising their hitting elbow parallel to shoulder level or slightly higher. This helps generate greater racquet speed in the contact zone—and thus greater power—by lengthening the downward arc of the racquet and facilitating more of a whipping motion on the swing. However, be warned that

SETTING UP ON THE FOREHAND

The hitter has his knees comfortably bent and will hit from an open stance because the ball is coming to him quickly (1). He tries to carry his racquet at around knee to midthigh height.

His feet remain planted (2) as he begins to draw the racquet up to a set position, with his hips and shoulders starting to rotate.

The racquet is up (3), ready to come down into the ball, and his hips and shoulders are prepared to uncoil into the shot from this solid position.

getting to this set position quickly, throughout a two-hour match, is directly related to the flexibility and strength in your hitting arm and shoulder.

If you've mastered a reliable stroke out of the traditional set position, with the elbow just below shoulder level, you can certainly hit with good power. But if you're serious about playing *power* racquetball, try moving to a higher setup off your basic foundation, while remembering your body limitations. I find that many younger players can crank their arm up easily, but as you age, you may need to do some moderate weight lifting and special flexibility exercises several times a week in order to take your arm and shoulder through the desired motion. (See photos of special drills in Chapter 11.)

When working on a quicker setup and/or the transition to a higher setup, be patient; it's going to take time to break ingrained habits and adjust to this new, foreign feeling. Since you'll tend to slip back into old comfortable patterns when you're playing a match, concentrate on this new motion in practice and off the court until it becomes a natural part of your overall swing. One helpful method is to get in front of a mirror and practice going back up and then down out of your set position (as compared to the photos in this book), so you can see the motion and get used to how it feels.

The Hitting Motion

You'll see top players with individual quirks on their setups and follow-throughs, but don't be misled: in between a full backswing and a complete finish—as they actually come down through the contact zone—they've all mastered the uncoiling, whipping action that generates maximum racquet speed as they contact the ball on as flat a plane as possible. The result is a velocity shot that travels low and straight to the front or side-wall target.

Try to visualize two basic concepts that must play off

The standard setup position (*left*) is highly effective in advanced play. However, power hitters—men and women alike—take the arm higher, with the elbow actually above the shoulder (*right*). This setup generates greater power by lengthening the arc of the stroke, but it requires strength and an efficient motion down into the ball.

each other as you swing: (1) a solidness of setup and (2) a suppleness of stroke. First, you want to have your knees comfortably bent and your feet planted, providing a sturdy base and leverage for your swing. Then take your racquet back up to a solid position—with the wrist cocked—and simultaneously start your downward motion, exploding into the ball. Drive the right side of your body into the shot, dipping the hitting shoulder, while the left side pulls through with the shoulder and hip rotating around and clearing the way for a clean, uncluttered stroke. Your goal is to have a fluid motion as you come down into the ball,

HITTING THE BALL

The hitter's wrist is cocked (1) and the racquet remains set as he starts coming down into the ball.

With the elbow still bent, the hitting shoulder dips to help get the racquet low into the shot (2). Notice the hip action and how the left arm is comfortably leading the way, helping to pull the body through the swing.

Now the hitter is getting into a side-arm-type swing (3), with the back knee bent and the hips pulling through.

The racquet is still laid back and the wrist is cocked an instant before impact (4). The hitter will now execute a natural whipping action through the contact zone.

This shows a typical follow-through, which may be shorter or longer depending upon the situation (5). The wrist has snapped through and the left arm has come around naturally, allowing the hitter full clearance with his hitting motion.

5

but working against a solid lower body so the racquet can have a whiplike action.

Another useful image is provided by Ben Hogan (the golfing great, not a member of the racquetball-playing family). He advises golfers to visualize themselves swinging inside a barrel so that they pivot their body over their power base and avoid lunging into the ball. This is a sound analogy for racquetball, since the forehand stroke is analogous to a golf swing. After you've stepped into the ball, strive to get good body rotation over your solid base—as though you were inside Hogan's imaginary barrel.

Contacting the Ball

Coming into impact, your swing should be leveling off so you can hit the ball on a flat plane toward your low-zone target area, resulting, ideally, in a shot that stays low when it hits and doesn't jump up after it takes its first bounce. Equally important, the wrist should still be cocked, the arm bent, and the racquet laid back. Then, in about the last 12 inches, there's an almost simultaneous sequence with the arm extending, the wrist snapping hard, and the racquet ripping through at impact. Concentrate on your wrist snap and the other desired actions in the contact zone will tend to fall in place.

When you have time to step into the ball as you go to hit (such as when you're given a "plum" off the front or side wall) give yourself leverage by planting your front foot and then starting down with the right side of your body. Ideally—when you step into the ball—try to make contact in that power gap off your front foot. But in a typical rally, of course, you're forced to contact the ball at different points between your two feet and, occasionally, even behind your back foot.

With experience, you'll learn to position your body against shots coming off a side wall or the back wall so that you can contact the ball at a prime height between calf and knee level. You may think you're hitting your setups at ankle height, but videotaping shows that we rarely contact the ball that low.

The Follow-Through

By completing your stroke with a full and forceful follow-through, you help insure that you come through the ball aggressively—the end result of a power forehand. In doing so, you also keep from letting your swing fizzle out or turn into a jabbing type of effort or end abruptly (which can possibly strain the arm). Instead, you're encouraged to develop a full swing, where you pick the ball up in the middle of that swing and drive it into your low-zone area without trying to "aim" it at a specific target.

In terms of how high you should actually finish with your racquet, just be flexible according to the basic stroke you develop. What counts is having the racquet go through the contact zone on a flat plane so that you maximize your chances of driving the ball low; then let the racquet come up naturally, between waist and shoulder level.

The Non-Hitting Arm

When you start down into the ball, full body rotation is crucial to what follows in utilizing the power in your body. You want to open up on the ball and hit through with nice freedom of motion by your right side, and this is made easier when you clear the left arm out of your way as you rotate the shoulder around. When your left arm is leading the way as you swing, the left shoulder can pull through freely, allowing the right side plenty of clearance to drive into the ball. You must get this body motion going—the left shoulder turning, the hip rotating—so that the forearm, the wrist, and the racquet face can come through in the right sequence.

So as you're analyzing your stroke (on your own, with the help of a friend, or by having yourself videotaped), check not only where your left hand is when you are setting up, but what your left arm is doing as you swing. Make sure it's not limiting the basic motion you seek. (Although this arm should lead your swing when you have time to set up and step into the shot, many times it will be tucked in against your chest to help provide balance when you're hitting while stretched out or on the run.

PULLING THE BALL DOWN FROM CHEST LEVEL

A refined skill among power hitters and advanced players is their ability to bring the ball down from around chest level into their low zone. Basically, this stroke is used

Pulling the ball down from chest level and hitting your low-zone area is a difficult skill, but one you'll need in advanced play, especially when you want to take the offensive against a short ceiling ball. Your opponent will have time to move into excellent coverage position, so work on stepping into the ball and having an efficient upper-body stroking motion.

against an opponent's ceiling-ball shot that comes in short and allows you an offensive shot. Instead of playing defensively by going back to the ceiling, top players take the offensive, either with a kill attempt or a passing shot that can put pressure on their opponent. This is definitely a power-type shot, requiring a solid base for leverage and a good swing with shoulder rotation, but it's one that should be tackled as your overall skill level rises.

You may already be thinking, "All the pros are pulling the ball down from around the chest and shoulder—I'd better work on that." Ideally, this will be a logical evolvement in your game, but first prove yourself at lower contact levels, working your way up from calf and knee level to waist level. When you can hit the ball efficiently from these levels into your low zone, then you're ready to go after higher shots.

CHAPTER 3

THE BACKHAND

Unless you have great compensating strengths, you can't expect to keep advancing in this game with a backhand that is basically a punching, directional shot. True, an excellent forehand can help shelter your ineffective backhand, allowing you to cover as much as four-fifths of the action zone with your forehand. Yet by taking this approach, you're banking all your hopes on the accuracy of one stroke—and eventually you're going to meet opponents who can direct the ball hard and tight along the side wall and force you to hit your backhand under continual pressure. Why limit your game—and your potential progress—by having such an exploitable area?

I know, of course, that few of us have a love affair with our backhand, and we recognize that fact in other players. When I ask students what they think about in terms of strategy for an important match, one of their main intentions is always: "Go to my opponent's backhand as often as I can." Then as I watch them play I notice that basically they're either afraid to hit out confidently with their backhand or they flail away recklessly with an all-or-nothing approach.

So let's go to work on a backhand you can swing with accuracy, a stroke that becomes an important weapon in your overall game, not one that is totally defensive or too often results in a skip.

THE GRIP

To switch grips from a conventional forehand to a conventional backhand (as I advocated in the previous chapter), move your hand slightly to the left on the racquet handle. Again, this provides a more natural and reliable way to come down through the ball with a vertical racquet face at impact—especially when using the wrist cock I recommend on the backswing. If you're having trouble with your backhand, and you hold the same grip off both sides (forehand and backhand), try learning to hit with the regular backhand grip shown on pages 44–45.

KEY ELEMENTS OF THE SWING

When you move toward your hitting position, think to yourself, "Shoulder the ball," and this will help set the desired sequence of actions in motion: (1) a full shoulder rotation to initiate the backswing, (2) a forceful but fluid shoulder motion into the ball, (3) strong hip rotation, (4) an extending of the arm and a snapping of the wrist in the contact zone, and (5) a complete follow-through.

Strive for an Early Setup
Just as on the forehand, it's crucial that you give yourself as much time as possible by having a quick, early backswing. Simply rotate your shoulders and hips toward the back wall and this will automatically set your racquet (with

THE BACKHAND SEQUENCE

The hitter will uncoil into the ball from this solid setup position (1). His knees are comfortably bent, the shoulders are rotated, the wrist is cocked, and the racquet is pulled back well above shoulder level.

Coming down into the ball, the hitting arm is still bent but starting to extend, the wrist is cocked, the back leg is bending, and the shoulders are rotating into the shot (2). This shoulder action gets the force of the body into the swing and pulls the racquet through the ball.

At impact off the front foot, the wrist is extended as it snaps through the hitting zone, generating significant additional power (3). Notice how the eyes are down on the ball and the body is in good balance, with the shoulders parallel to the side wall and the left arm trailing the swing.

When you have time and the proper clearance from your opponent, strive to finish with a smooth, complete follow-through (4); stopping abruptly can strain the shoulder.

your hitting arm bent at the elbow and the wrist fully cocked), allowing you to now uncoil naturally into the ball. Just make sure you're taking your racquet back far enough and high enough to insure full swing expansion and good shoulder rotation into the shot. (If you set your racquet early, but you still find yourself "arming" the ball, check that you're actually getting your shoulders into action. With little or no shoulder rotation, you can't utilize the power of your upper body and the best you can do is swing hard and punch at the ball with your arm, which results in arm fatigue as you play a tough match, less velocity, and greater inaccuracy. This excessive strain can also lead to a sore arm.)

Once you feel comfortable hitting from this basic set position, you may be tempted to emulate some of the pros

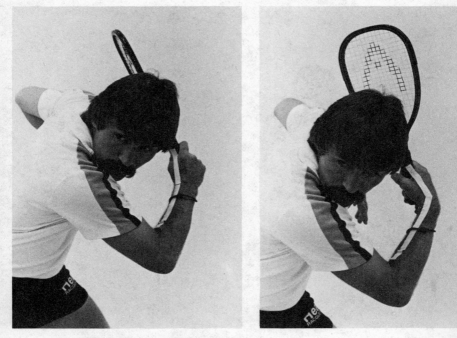

THE WRIST-COCK POSITIONS

On the standard setup position *(left),* the wrist is cocked up, with the hand basically on line with the forearm. Mastering a wrist snap out of this position is much easier than the "curl" backhand and there's less chance for error at impact.

Although some pros like to curl the wrist back *(right),* this introduces a difficult timing problem. The racket face turns significantly on the setup, forcing adjustments as you curl back in and try to have the racquet face *parallel* to the front wall when you contact the ball (and not slightly tilted down or up).

by curling the wrist (that is, wrapping the palm back toward the inside of your forearm.) This extreme wrist cock can look and feel like it is generating greater power, but beware: *it takes expert timing to get out of this corkscrew position and still hit with power and, most important, accuracy.* The pros who do this have swings that have been grooved through many years of playing virtually every day. Yet I find that most all other players have horrendous problems trying to incorporate this little technique into their swings. So my advice would be: refine the stroke you have, using the standard wrist cock, and concentrate on getting more efficient shoulder action, for this is where the *real power* is derived on the backhand.

Shoulder Rotation

Remember, there's nothing to impede your swing on the backhand—physiologically—so get into that rhythm of rotating your shoulders back and then unwinding into the shot. Although the stroke you seek is clean and compact, you also want an open, free-flowing motion as you snap the racquet through the impact zone and finish all the way around. In rotating your shoulders, make sure to dip your front shoulder low enough to enable your head to move freely while your eyes remain glued to the ball.

Realistically, you'll almost always have all you can handle just setting up and getting through on the ball without being jammed. But when your opponent's shot gives you extra time, don't "jump" at the ball in your overeagerness for the kill. Tell yourself, "Wait on the ball and shoulder it," so that you're rotating over your power base as you transfer your weight into the shot.

Contacting the Ball

When you set up strongly with the shoulders rotated back, the hitting elbow comfortably bent, and the wrist cocked, visualize a rubber band being pulled back—and

1 **2**

now released as you start your forward motion into the ball. Coming into the contact zone (12 to 18 inches before impact), you're pulling through with the shoulder, the arm is beginning to extend, and the racquet is trailing. Then, almost simultaneously, you want your arm to extend fully—popping into the ball—while the wrist is snapping at impact. This is what delivers maximum velocity to your shots. Meanwhile, the racquet should be coming through on a horizontal plane with the face straight up and down at impact, since you're trying to drive the ball low and hard. Stay down through the shot to avoid inadvertently lifting the ball.

BODY-ROTATION DRILL

To practice the desired body rotation on the backswing (1), start by facing the side wall, hands on hips.

Rotate toward the back wall (2) with your eyes remaining focused on the intended point of impact.

Take the same motion with a racquet in your hand (3). Notice how the body should be comfortably coiled—over a solid base—before you swing down through the ball.

MUTUAL RESPECT IN CENTER-COURT

Properly played, there's a mutual respect for one's opponent in racquetball that minimizes the chances of injury and leads to more enjoyable play. One example is to have adaptable follow-throughs on the backhand that take into account where your opponent is positioned as you hit.

When he gets caught close to your right side during a tough center-court rally, and you have him momentarily blocked out of the play (1), learn to hit with a shortened follow-through so you can make the appropriate scoring shot.

In a similar situation (2), when you have a little room, take a longer swing and hit with full shoulder rotation. But, as shown here, pull your racquet up on the follow-through, safely avoiding your opponent.

The Follow-Through

A common problem on backhands is a plain lack of confidence, which leads players to stop their racquet out in front of the body—the end result of a punch stroke (and also a jerking action that puts added strain on the elbow). Instead of this hesitant approach, concentrate on a follow-through that takes you all the way around after you hit, completing the aggressive motion you want to master. You'll find that when you strive to finish like this—with the hitting arm coming through freely after impact—you tend to also take a full swing from the beginning.

The Non-Hitting Arm

If you already have an excellent swing, then touching your non-hitting hand to the racquet handle as you start your backswing is not likely affecting your efficiency. However, this is a superfluous habit that may be keeping you from bringing your racquet back quickly enough or far enough and can also limit your shoulder rotation. You may be unaware that you're doing this, so have a friend watch as you play (or use videotaping). As for the non-hitting arm, hold it in a comfortable position where it doesn't inhibit a full extension of your swing—either at your side or brought up parallel with the racket arm. Taking the arm up may help you swing with a more fluid motion, but it also requires extra energy.

Many top players hold their left arm close to the body as they swing—out of habit or for better balance and rhythm. Others prefer to take this arm up in tandem with the hitting arm, as shown (p. 49). Use whichever style gives you the best results with your stroking motion.

DEVELOPING AN AGGRESSIVE APPROACH

Along with developing a solid stroke that you can rely on under pressure, you may find that you need a more aggressive attitude on the backhand. In practice, for example, just concentrate on turning your shoulders into the shot and ripping away, regardless if the ball hits a foot high on the front wall or 10 feet. Get that nice feeling of hearing the ball pop against the wall and gain the confidence that you can hit the ball hard—then go to work on also hitting your low-zone targets. In practice matches, try to take a healthy swing at the ball when you have an offensive opportunity, knowing that even if you miss your target—assuming you avoid skipping the ball—your power can still give you a possible ace in the hole. You may end up driving the ball past an opponent who has position ahead of you, or it may come to him hard, at difficult angles, and at least force him to execute a good shot to win the rally. (In tournament and league play, use good discretion when using this aggressive backhand.)

CHAPTER 4

ADAPTABLE FORM

At every level of play, racquetball technique goes on as a struggle somewhere between the real and the ideal. Stepping into the ball and having good "textbook" form may be in the back of your mind as you cover the court, but when the ball is screeching straight at you off the front wall 22 feet away, or caroming past you down a side wall, or heading into a back corner, what counts is how well you can return the ball with what I call "adaptable form." Basically, you still want to try to score from these positions, but if that's not possible, then at least you want to minimize the setups you give your opponent—by having an efficient upper-body swing from different footwork positions.

MASTERING AN UPPER-BODY SWING

To make adaptable form work, you can't take an attitude that "anything goes" with your technique. Even though you'll often get caught in different stances, unable to step into the ball, you'll nearly always have time to ex-

Notice how the hitter stretches for the ball by taking a long cross-over step with his left leg and then extends his racquet arm while using shoulder rotation and a wrist snap to hit the ball offensively. His opponent is in a good coverage position, watching the ball and ready to cover the shot if it's left up.

ecute a quick upper-body stroke. So learn how to position yourself in such a way that your upper body and hips can move freely through the shot, however your feet are positioned. Then instead of simply "arming" the ball in desperation, you'll be utilizing the whipping action that results when you get your shoulders into the shot, a wrist snap in the contact zone, and ideally some hip rotation. When you have a quick stroke like this, you'll find that you don't need to step into the ball in fast-action exchanges in order to hit with good direction and velocity.

HITTING FROM AN "OPEN" STANCE

In almost any extended rally, you'll be forced to hit from variations of an open stance, where you're either facing the front wall with both feet as the ball approaches or your feet are widened out toward a front corner. Although your feet are basically planted, generally you only have time to react to a shot that is heading into your body or threatening to get past you. What counts, therefore, is your ability to quickly set your racquet and swing through the best you can.

Work at expanding the area you can cover out of your open stance without having to take a step, for this is critical in a low-zone exchange with your opponent. In recent years I've widened my hitting base by spreading my legs a little further apart when I see the ball coming and I know I'm not going to have time for any extra body positioning. I feel like I now have a stronger swing in a wider area and that I can stretch out and hit with a clean, forceful stroke by pulling or driving through with good shoulder action. Knee bend is also crucial here, along with the ability to dip your hitting shoulder to get the racquet low for those potential winners that come to you only 6 inches off the floor.

Many times you'll be forced to hit from an open stance, with your feet planted and pointed toward the front wall or into the front corner. From here, you must swing with a compact stroke that relies on your upper body and as much hip rotation as time and your positioning allows.

When you're caught in an open stance, a hard, well-angled passing shot will occasionally force you to contact the ball behind your back foot. The left arm will sometimes be held against your body for balance when you're reaching out to hit like this.

HITTING WHEN STRETCHED OUT OR ON THE RUN

When the ball is out away from your body, forcing you to stretch wide or to hit while on the move, your form is not going to look picturesque, but no matter: *you must learn to be efficient with these shots.* Either try to score if the situation dictates, try to drive the ball if you can't go for an all-out winner, or flip the ball to the ceiling if you're totally on the defensive.

If you're digging the ball up in the service box area or thrusting over to a side wall, there's a technique you can work on: stretching out with your legs, then a reaching with your hitting arm, and then a snapping action with your wrist.

There's a tendency for players to think that anything hit while on the run should just be flipped back to the front wall to keep the rally going, but you'll find yourself capitalizing on scoring opportunities if you've worked on hitting with the free-flowing, upper-body swing described above. Many top players can't hit winners while on the run, but they have the ability to hit excellent passing shots—and the sense to flip the ball smartly to the ceiling to get a better foothold in the rally when they're on the defensive.

Although we're forced to hit while on the run throughout a match, I've found that few players ever actually practice this technique. Yet this is something you can do easily by yourself. Just throw the ball out away from you and then go after it, hitting with a whipping shoulder rotation as you're moving. You can also have a partner bounce or drive the ball deep into areas that force you to scramble for the ball.

In this sequence, the defender is studying his opponent's stroke, then moving forward quickly to cover his left-up kill attempt. Notice how much court he can cover by taking two long strides and then stretching forward with his racquet extended to either re-kill the ball or dig it up and keep it in play. ▶

CHAPTER 5

THE SERVE

Good serving is built upon many individual approaches: your location in the service box, your step motion into the ball, your stroke, and your method of relocation. Yet in striving for an expert serve there's not some unique overall style you must uncover, achievable only by the pros. This chapter will give you the key guidelines that you can actually tackle on your own in practice. Then, as you play, there's always an objective measurement of your effectiveness: *how consistently you can get the ball deep into the back corners* and, by doing so, either (1) have the possibility of an ace, (2) force a weak return, or (3) cause your opponent to go defensively to the ceiling. Conversely, you want to minimize his good offensive opportunities by keeping the ball from coming off the walls as a setup.

THE LOW-DRIVE SERVE

Build your attack around this serve, for when you can make the ball bounce just beyond the short line—between you and the side wall, on the floor—*you will neutralize the best of opponents.* Of course, applying this pressure demands pinpoint accuracy as you try to hit front-wall target areas that are much smaller than commonly visualized. I've found, for example, that I'm aiming for a rectangular target about 4 inches high and 9 inches wide. If I hit slightly lower, the serve is short; if I'm slightly higher, the ball rebounds off the back wall for a setup. This target area is about the same size for most advanced players, but its location up and down will vary—depending upon the velocity of your serve and how low you can get your racquet into the shot so that you can hit with a slight upward stroke, giving the ball an arc to safely clear the short line.

Beginners can aim for larger targets because their opponents lack the ability to capitalize as often on serves that are hit either too high or at too wide an angle. But in tougher competition, the premium is on accuracy; your target areas must shrink and you must hit them more frequently, since your opponents can put away many more of your misses or certainly force you onto the defensive. You're trying to give your opponent minimum reaction time, but more important, you want to pin him deep along the side walls and in the back corners without allowing him a chance to set up.

Find Your Front-Wall Targets

If you've been relying on instinct and experience to sense where you should hit the front wall, it's unlikely that you can point to your actual low-drive targets. Not to worry if you've developed a great serve, but when inconsistency is a big problem—as it is for most players—here's an easy method to determine your exact target areas in practice.

As you serve, have a friend stand near the front wall (safely to one side) and mark where the ball hits this wall, while you watch the path of the ball so you can categorize the serve as short, good, or long. Ideally, if you use peel-off

These are your important front-wall targets on the serve, when contacting the ball from the middle of the court. Remember that when you readjust your position in either direction, these targets will all shift accordingly and, because of the angles involved, some of them will be eliminated—either because your location will make them impossible to hit or to avoid being guilty of a screen.

The targets for your hard, aggressive serves are shown large *(top)* for purposes of illustration.

In reality, to be effective in advanced play, you must hit target areas that are approximately 4-by-9 inches in size *(bottom)*.

stickers in three different colors to mark the corresponding spots on the wall, you'll soon have a visual target area outlining where you want to hit. (Remember that an excellent serve either takes two bounces before the back wall or hits the floor correctly and barely nicks the side wall. In either case, the ball doesn't come off either wall as a setup.)

Once you've established your target areas from a particular contact position in the service box, you still must rely on "feel" when you actually play a match. But you'll develop a sounder serve and one that causes you far less anxiety under pressure if you spend time getting that relationship fixed between where you contact the ball and the target area. Then instead of relying on guesswork to make adjustments, you can be objective. "Even though I now realize just how small my targets are, I know *where* they are and I actually serve better," said a friend. "I concentrate more on what I'm doing and if I'm missing, I know it's just a matter of hitting a couple of inches higher or lower on the front wall. So I get a lot less frustrated with myself."

Footwork Motion in the Service Box

Good serving (on low-drives and hard "Z's") starts with a two-step motion into the ball that covers as much of the 5-foot service box as you can comfortably manage. This helps generate maximum leg power and upper-body momentum into the shot. As the photographs show, the first step is usually a short preparation step by the right foot, perhaps 12 inches straight or diagonally toward the front wall, followed by a long power stride with the left leg. Contact the ball off your front foot, from calf to just above knee level, depending upon how low you can get (by bending your back knee and bending at the waist or dipping your hitting shoulder) in order to hit slightly up at the ball. Here's where you also want solid forehand technique—a whipping swing and an explosive wrist snap in the impact zone.

THE TWO-STEP MOTION

(Left) Ready to begin his motion into the ball, the server has his feet on the short line so that he can use the entire 5-foot service zone.

(Right) The first step is normally about 12 inches, in this case just a back cross-over step, but there are many variations.

This short preparatory step is followed by a long powerful stride forward, setting up the ideal forehand stroke. The server plants the left foot and comes through with all his power.

Relocation After Serving

Relocation is an easy and natural shuffling motion to deep court when your opponent goes to the ceiling. However, if he tries to go low zone with your serve, relocation becomes much tougher because of the minimal time involved. This is a crucial skill, but one that too often is neglected by advancing players, which greatly limits their progress. Remember: racquetball is played primarily in the back half of the court, and you can't afford to remain in the service box thinking you can handle the well-placed returns of an opponent. Work hard to reach as solid a covering position as time allows—ideally, 3 or 4 feet behind the back service line—knowing that there will still be many times when your opponent stretches over and returns the ball offensively before you're ready.

Trying to relocate properly behind the service box, after serving aggressively, is one of the toughest jobs in racquetball. Your momentum is going forward as you land on your left foot, and now you must bank and go the other way as quickly as possible by driving off your left leg while pivoting with your right leg. Maintaining good body control through all of this is equally important, since you want to be ready to break in any direction to cover your opponent's return. Try to relocate close to the middle of the court (between the side walls), shading just slightly to the side your opponent is on, but giving him clearance to hit down-the-line or cross-court.

For a low-drive serve, the ball should be hit on a slightly upward arc, allowing it to be hit hard while safely carrying the short line. The server is contacting the ball about 6 to 8 inches off the floor and aiming for a front-wall target about 18 inches high (as indicated by the yardstick).

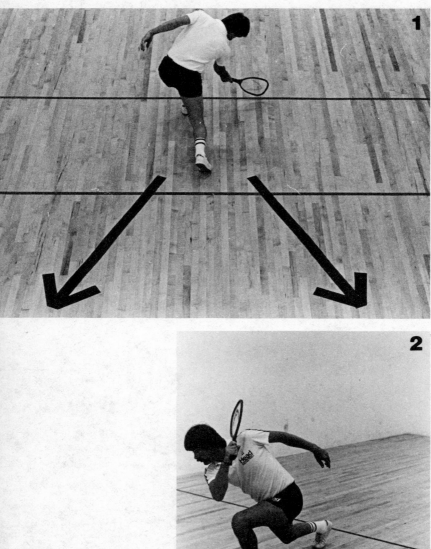

RELOCATING AFTER THE SERVE

When the server snaps the ball properly into a back corner, he should relocate diagonally back, as indicated by the arrows (1). If he misses his target to either side, he may have to adjust straight back or move to the other side of the court.

He stays low as he completes a powerful stroke, while maintaining good body balance (2).

Quick and efficient movement out of the service box starts with this simultaneous action—pivoting on the right foot and driving back with the left leg (3).

Try to get your left foot back as far as possible (4), while studying your opponent's intentions.

A long shuffle step (5) will now move you far enough back hopefully to avoid being jammed by an opponent's quick low-zone return.

If you see that your opponent is going to the ceiling (6), retreat to the back of the court, where her shot is going to locate.

If your opponent is going low zone (7), anchor down as you try to read his return—and be ready to move.

After serving, immediately look back to see the path of the ball, and then study your opponent to see whether he's going low zone or high zone. "Reading" his intentions right up until impact will give you invaluable information as you anticipate your next shot. Conversely, if you turn back to the front wall before your opponent goes to hit, you've reached a plateau in your improvement because you have *no anticipation.*

Other Low-Drive Reminders

Two strategy points on the low drive:

1. Since it's difficult for players at every level to be consistently accurate with this serve, use it only as a first attempt. And if you're going to error, try to error on the short side. You still have an effective second serve that can safely neutralize your opponent (either "Z's" or lobs) and meanwhile you're not giving him plums off the back and side walls.

2. I emphasize having the ball hit the floor first because this heads the ball on a good angle toward the back corner. It may go directly to the corner, or—ideally—carom slightly off the side wall and then into the corner. (As the photos show, a deep side-wall nick off the floor can force your opponent to stretch another 9 to 12 inches for his return, and this can often mean the difference in getting his racquet on the ball.) You may be tempted to gamble for "crack" aces by trying to have the ball catch the juncture between the side wall and the floor, but it's rarely worth the risk (nor is it even a realistic expectation). If you happen to get this ace, fine, but don't count on it happening when it's 8–all in a tiebreaker. More important, when the ball hits the side wall directly off the front wall, it will almost always kick out toward the middle of the court, giving your opponent an offensive shot.

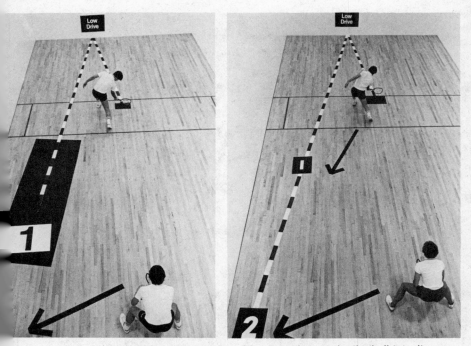

Your best percentage goal on a low-drive serve is to make the ball take its first bounce within the black rectangle *(left)*—ideally, just behind the short line. The ball will then carry into the back corner and force your opponent to stretch out just to get his racquet on the ball.

This low-drive angle has the ball traveling straight into the back corner *(right)*, landing between the server and the side wall and bouncing twice before reaching the back wall.

Low
Drive

2

Many times an even more effective serve is to try to have the ball barely nick the side wall on its way to the back corner. This can force the returner to stretch an extra foot, which is often enough to cause a weaker return. Unfortunately, this serve oftentimes catches too much side wall and comes off as a setup.

THE "CRACK" ACE ATTEMPT

Some players are tempted to bring the serve in just beyond the short line and close to the junction of the floor and the side wall, hoping for a "crack" ace or a ball that bounces twice before the returner can move forward to dig it up.

Unfortunately, this serve is much more likely to catch the side wall too high and then carom directly into the returner.

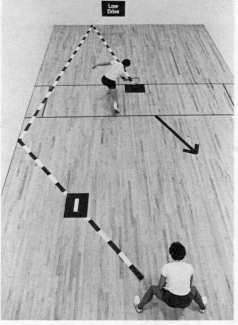

When the crack ace attempt fails, notice where the server must relocate to give his opponent open hitting lanes to the front wall (leaving himself particularly vulnerable to a down-the-line pass).

THE "Z" SERVE

You've played the game long enough to know how important it is to have an aggressive "Z" serve that causes your opponent grief by traveling deep and tight into both back corners. I'm also sure you've often paid the penalty for missing your desired front-wall targets. So here again, practicing alone and with a friend will enable you to find those exact targets that yield the ideal pattern: front wall, side wall, floor, opposite side wall—and keep the ball off the back wall as a setup. Although this pattern is more crucial to success than velocity, always try to combine both for increased difficulty. First master hitting your front-wall targets, practicing with different balls (pressurized and pressureless) and at different speeds to see how they tend to react off the last side wall; then work on improving your pace within that pattern.

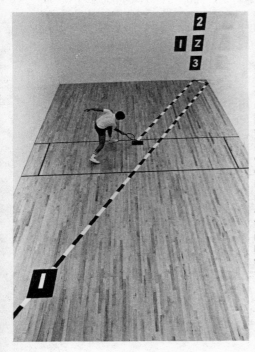

The lines on the court indicate the path this "Z" serve will take when properly executed, with the first bounce occuring deep and close to the opposite side wall. The numbers on the front wall represent incorrect target areas. A ball striking Area 1 will angle more down the middle of the court and carom off the back wall, then the side wall—coming off as a setup for your opponent. If the ball hits Area 2, it will follow the correct "Z" path but come off the back wall as a setup. Area 3 is too low; the ball will take its desired path but come in short of the back wall, allowing the returner to hit an offensive return.

The properly executed "Z" will take its first bounce on the floor, then carom into the side wall and (if allowed to go past) will ideally take its second bounce before coming off the back wall.

In terms of positioning, most players are discovering that it's easier, safer, and equally effective to move a few feet to either side of center to hit. This shifts the front-wall targets farther away from the side wall, making them easier to see and diminishing the fear of hitting the side wall first.

When practicing, learn to read the ball as it comes off the front wall so that you have a good idea where to relocate as you move back—particularly if you've hit short and you sense that your opponent is going to move up and cut the ball off after it bounces and before it reaches the side wall. Also be ready to give him the proper hitting lanes for his cross-court kill or pass attempt should the ball jump off the side wall for a set up.

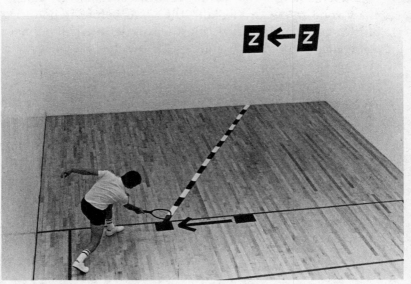

If you move off to the left to hit your "Z" serve, just remember that your target has to move accordingly.

THE LOB SERVES

These serves are mandatory not simply as safe second attempts, but either to introduce a deliberate style of play that may get the rally started in your favor or to change the pace of the game or the match.

The Half-Lob Serve

The half-lob has actually become an important tactical weapon in the power game, thanks to a rule change since my first book. There's now a 5-foot zone behind the service box and, in tournament play, the returner loses the point if the referee judges that his racquet has entered that imaginary zone trying to "fly-kill" the serve before it bounces. Instead of taking that risk, most players let the ball bounce, and since a good lob bounces up around shoulder level, a ceiling return usually is dictated.

In most situations, try to have the half-lob serve land within the 5-foot zone behind the service box, for it will then arc toward the back wall and carry into the returner's hitting area around shoulder level, usually dictating a ceiling-ball return.

Therefore, your goal is to have this serve land in the 5-foot zone or slightly beyond, a strategy that many times neutralizes the power player. (The half-lob "Z" generates the same ceiling return by taking a high bounce and kicking into your opponent about shoulder height.) Also, as much as you want to serve aggressively to keep your opponent off-balance when he hits, there are days when your execution is shaky and his returns are crisp and accurate, putting you constantly on the defensive. Here's where you can't be shy about changing your strategy and going to your half-lob; at least you'll get safely into the rally.

Neither lob serve requires any real footwork—just a nice comfortable stroke, with or without a step into the ball. This is a direction shot, so keep your wrist basically firm as you swing, and concentrate on an easy shoulder and arm motion. You'll bring on too many problems, especially under pressure, if you try to flick your wrist to generate speed on this shot.

Directionally, keep this serve off the side wall, but try to keep it close to the wall and into the back corners. The ball is traveling so slow that any contact with the side wall will send it out as an absolute plum for your opponent.

The High-Lob Serve

Hit this serve with the same easy but secure arm and shoulder motion, so you're not dependent on wrist action. Ideally, try to have the ball graze the side wall at about 35 feet as it comes down. This keeps the ball close to that wall and pushes your opponent deep into the corner. The danger, of course, is that the slightest error on your part will cause the ball to either catch too much of the side wall and carom out toward the middle of the court, or simply miss the side wall and rebound straight off the back wall for a setup.

THE SECOND SERVE

Since many of your low-drive first serves will be landing short, don't slight your second serves in practice. And when you play, enamored as you might be with the power game, keep two basic goals in mind:

Effective high-lobs land deeper in the court (as shown here) or graze the side wall on their descent. However, they can also take their first bounce just behind the service box, providing the ball has been hit to the front wall on a very high arc.

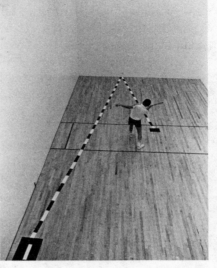

The high "Z" lob is an increasingly popular off-speed serve, thanks to the current 5-foot rule on service returns. Top players fear breaking the imaginary plane if they try to volley or short-hop this serve, so they let it bounce and usually go up to the ceiling with their return.

1. *Go with a second serve you know you can easily get in play.* Why gamble with a side-out and simply hand the serve back to your opponent by trying a low-drive under this added pressure? Instead, work on hitting a controlled "Z" or an accurate lob.

2. *Avoid giving your opponent an offensive opportunity.* Your best choices here again will be the controlled "Z" and the different lobs, since both serves get the ball in play with more ease, while coming into your opponent's hitting zone at about shoulder height.

CAMOUFLAGING YOUR SERVE

Camouflaging your intended serves (low-drives and hard "Z's") is important at top levels of play, since deception costs your opponent split seconds in anticipation and can thus lead to weaker returns and more setups. However, first master a basic two-step motion into the ball—and groove your front-wall targets—or you may only fool yourself with tricky ploys. This one motion can actually take you a long way, but in tougher competition you may need to develop a second and third footwork style in order to keep opponents off-balance. At the pro level, I'm forced to hit the same serves out of different motions because opponents can easily groove into one motion and begin to time my hit.

One common strategy, for example, is to take your low-drive motion to the left, but pound the ball down the right wall for a possible ace or to draw a weak return. Or, come off that motion to the left but instead of hitting a low-drive down the left wall, snap a hard "Z" that travels to the opposite back right corner. The key, of course, is to make the right adjustments in your front-wall targets and to execute properly. Let's say that your "Z" to the backhand corner has been working well, and you sense that your op-

When you move away from the middle of the court to serve, you may eliminate one of your "Z" options. By moving to the right, the server here can hit low-drives to both back corners and a "Z" to his opponent's forehand, but he creates a virtually impossible angle for hitting a "Z" to the backhand corner.

ponent is leaning toward that corner as you go to hit. This will make the low-drive down the right wall—using the same motion—much more effective. Don't be afraid to use strategies like this; you'll need all of them and more against advanced players.

STRATEGY ON THE SERVE

Here are some tactics that may help make your serve more effective:

- Think before you go to serve. Having your serve in mind as you enter the service box will free you to concentrate on your target area as you catch your breath.
- Don't lose your concentration if your opponent is using the 10-second rule by holding his racquet up in the air as you're preparing to start your step motion. In a tournament, ask the referee to explain his interpretation of the rule if you feel your opponent is using it to deliberately and unfairly slow down play—but don't get flustered; just accept it as a part of this particular match.
- Most of your serves will likely go into your opponent's backhand corner (normally his weaker side), but *don't ignore the virtues of good forceful serves to his forehand.* First of all, this keeps your opponent from "cheating" to his backhand side—mentally, in anticipation, if not physically. If you're always attacking the backhand, his readiness will help compensate for this weaker stroke. Second, he may not be accustomed to moving right and effectively returning your tough serves. A "Z," especially, that is snapped quickly into the right corner might handcuff him before he can get properly set up for his return.
- Against most good opponents, you must vary your serves as the match progresses, but when your opponent has a definite weaker side (forehand or backhand), exploit that area the best you can and keep the screws tightened.

● Avoid predictability in your serve selection and direction. Mix up your serves—with a purpose in mind—so that your opponent doesn't gain an important edge in anticipation, where he's "seeing" the ball coming before you even hit it. I used to hit all of my first serves at the same hard pace, but eventually I realized that my effectiveness was diminishing as the match progressed, with many of my opponents teeing off on their returns. I've since become a smarter server and I'm not a mechanical machine who says, "I will simply try to outhit you." Today when I'm playing, I'll serve aggressively, then change the pace with slower "Z's" and half-lobs. I'm always looking for ways to get my opponent out of his rhythm and cause some weaker returns. Also, I keep moving around in the service box so he's constantly seeing something a little different. If one serve isn't working, I'll move to a new spot and try the same serve but from a different angle. In doing this yourself, however, remember: you must have a good feel for your different target areas, for they will be constantly changing in relation to where you contact the ball.

● Let's say you're in a knock-down match, midway through the second game, and you've been mixing your serves up, but your opponent is hot and nothing is working effectively. What's a possible solution, short of simply getting better execution of your serves? My final approach is to focus on what I feel is my opponent's biggest weakness, since it has the greatest chance of breaking down under persistent pressure. Maybe his weakness hasn't surfaced yet, but I know if I can keep pounding away, I may finally begin to get the slightly weaker returns I need. And when I get these scoring opportunities, I know I have to capitalize on them. So what it may come down to, late in the second game or the tiebreaker, is this: play the percentages by serving to your opponent's most exploitable area, because it will probably break down the quickest with time running out and the pressure mounting.

THE PROBLEM OF SCREEN SERVES

Screen serves are illegal, and they hurt the spirit of the game, but many players (including myself) have learned to hit them, taking advantage of a rule that is difficult to interpret and enforce. Basically, the rule states that the returner must have full view of the ball before it passes the server's body. (In reality, we're talking about low-drives hit from several areas in the service box.) Technically, there

SCREEN SERVES

Screen serves usually only come into play on low-drives, where the ball is hit low enough into the front wall for the server to block the returner's view of the ball. This is a subjective ruling in most cases, and one of the hardest interpretations in racquetball today.

Hitting from the middle of the court, the server illegally screens the returner's view of the ball as it comes off the front wall.

Moving off to the left, the server is denying his opponent a good view of the ball before it passes by his body.

The returner appears to have a clear view of the ball here, but is often screened when the server steps in this direction.

must be at least 18 inches between the server's body and the ball, to either side—but who can actually determine this margin when the ball is traveling 100 miles an hour or faster? Obviously interpretation enters in, along with inconsistency and controversy when a referee is doing the interpreting.

Screens may not be a problem in day-to-day matches around the club if you and your opponents try to play the game fairly, with a mutual respect for two basic rules: (1) the returner should be able to see the serve before it passes the server's body, and (2) the returner should not have to move his position in order to see the serve. Unfortunately, screens can cause considerable bickering in league and tournament play, where some players try to bend the rules as much as humanly possible.

PRACTICE AND EVALUATION TIPS

1. You don't need a lot of time to work on your serve—perhaps just 10 minutes out of a practice session or before you go to play a match—but practice hard. Remember: precision and consistency in hitting your target areas are absolutely crucial.

2. Set aside time by yourself on the court to concentrate on mastering the total movement: your two-step motion (on low-drives and hard "Z's"), hitting your target area, and then relocating quickly and in good control—visualizing an opponent's low-zone return or defensive ceiling return.

3. Practice your two-step motion in front of a mirror so you can see the actual movements involved (as compared to the photos in this chapter). You can even mark off a 5-foot area in your living room or the back yard and then rehearse the motion without a ball.

4. Try to have part of one of your matches videotaped

and you'll see for yourself just how effectively you're re-locating to a position where you're as ready as possible to cover your opponent's return. In your mind you may think you're efficient—until you see yourself on the television screen. If you notice that you're slow getting back, this may be the reason why you're constantly being jammed or easily passed by an opponent's low-zone returns. (Of course, a friend can also watch for these things as you play.)

5. Put black tape on the front wall to mark your de-sired low-drive and "Z" targets when hitting from a specific location in the service box. Then try to groove your foot-work motion and your stroke so that you contact the ball in the same relationship to your target as often as possible.

6. When you begin serving from different positions in the service box, and at different angles, remember that

Notice how the server's low-drive target moves significantly to the right in relationship to his new hitting position.

geometry is at work and you must do your homework in practice by recalculating your targets. Getting all your front-wall targets fixed in your mind takes diligence and concentration, but this is a fact of life for advanced players.

7. Practice hitting all your serves into both back corners so that you have a flexible attack for different types of opponents, especially that left-hander you always seem to face in the quarterfinals or semifinals.

8. Evaluate your serving accuracy. Your low-drive may *sound* great as it booms off the front wall, but when you objectively study it—by measuring fifty low-drives in practice or by having a friend chart one of your matches—you may discover that a high percentage are actually coming off the walls as setups. The same attention should be given to all your serves.

CHAPTER 6

RETURNING SERVE

Trying to get a rally started against a skillful server is obviously a challenging task. On his first serve, you can never really predict what he's going to hit, since he'll be diversifying his serves, ripping a low-drive to your backhand corner one time, then snapping a hard "Z" to your forehand. Moreover, he gives you minimum time to react by camouflaging his intentions the best he can and screening the ball—within the rules—so you may not get a full view of the ball until just before it passes by his body. Nor will you be hitting from the same footwork position serve after serve: some low drives will go straight in to the back corner, others will just nick the side wall, and others will come shooting off into your body. The same applies for "Z's" hit with varying speed.

At times, returning the ball in advanced play has to come down to native strength and stretching ability as you extend your body out toward the side wall to dig up a low-drive. Yet there's much you can do to maximize the talent you already have by working on your efficiency in moving to the ball, your shot selection, and your execution.

MOVING TO THE BALL

Since I want to be able to break easily in any direction, I await serve about a long stride off the back wall, midway between the side walls, with my weight evenly distributed. I hold a backhand grip (because the majority of balls come to our backhand) but I avoid leaning in that direction.

Standing relatively close to the back wall (1) gives you slightly more reaction time to reach a low-drive serve into either back corner and (2) enables you to move laterally rather than back on a diagonal, which forces you to hit while actually moving away from the front wall. It's okay to stand a little further forward (5 to 6 feet from the back wall) if your opponent's low-drives and hard "Z's" are continually popping off the walls as setups. But don't try to take a position almost halfway to the short line, thinking this will help you cover crack ace attempts that land just beyond the short line. This serve is Fantasyland, even in the pro game, and is going to occur far less often than an opponent's deep serves that force you to retreat—not to mention the low-drives that can get past you more easily for aces when you're positioned too far forward.

Mentally, you should be studying the server's motion, trying to determine what he's going to hit—and where. Against a power hitter who has good accuracy, and when playing with a live ball, some players might advise you to gamble on the first serve by simply breaking right or left in anticipation of a low-drive to the corner. But this is to play too much of a hit-or-miss type of game. I feel it's better to simply accept the occasional ace and concentrate on being ready to capitalize on those numerous low-drives he keeps popping off the back wall.

Covering the Low-Drive Serve

Returns off the low-drive generally fall into these categories:

First, when the serve has been hit crisply and is going to stay tight along the side wall without coming off the back wall, you must learn to move over into the corner with a cross-over step, a long stretch, and then an extended reach with your racquet. This cross-over step is essential in advanced play, for there's simply not enough time to take quick shuffle steps to get to the corner. Strive for a controlled movement toward the side wall so that even when you're stretched out, you can take the ball accurately up to the ceiling, pushing your opponent back while preventing the ace or the weak return.

Second, if the serve is going to stay off the back wall but is away from the side wall, your initial movement to the corner may be a cross-over step, then a stride into the ball, and a strong, forceful swing. Or, you may prefer to take quick shuffle steps to get into hitting position. Whatever, this is an easier ball to reach and you can oftentimes be offensive with your return. When the ball comes even more into the middle, you may only have to readjust your feet and rotate your body before taking a solid swing.

Third, when the serve is hit off-target and kicks off one or two walls as a setup, you can use a variety of foot repositions to get behind the ball and then go for a scoring shot. Even the best of servers have trouble hitting hard low-drives that consistently burrow into the back corner, so be ready for more setups than you may realize—and don't be afraid or unprepared to take the offensive.

Covering the "Z" Serve

The key here, through playing experience and practice sessions, is to learn to read this serve as it is angling diagonally across the court toward the side wall. Then you can make your shot-selection decisions without any real need for panic.

● If the "Z" is going to be good (contacting the front

THE LOW-DRIVE RETURN

Unusual as it may look, many players hold this ready position until the server starts his movement into the ball.

Sensing a low-drive serve, the returner now moves into a lower ready position (by widening his stance and bending his knees), which facilitates moving efficiently to either corner.

Forced to move quickly to the deep corner, the returner takes a long cross-over step with his right leg as he pulls the racquet back for the hit.

Stretched out with his body, and his arm extended, he relies on good shoulder action and a wrist snap to hit the best return he can manage.

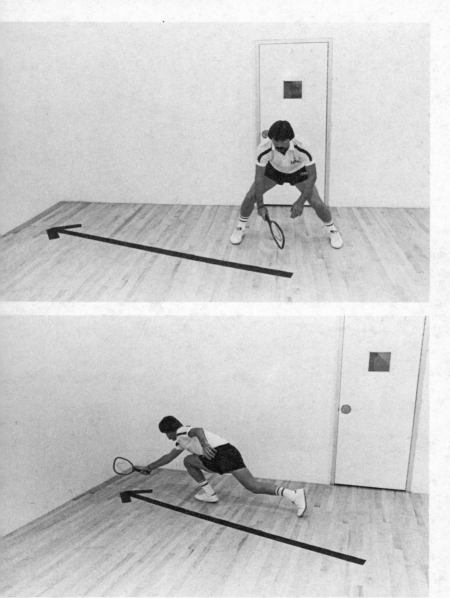

Notice the same principles at work when the defender must extend out to his forehand corner to reach a serve that goes tight along the side wall.

and side wall at the correct angle and height), you must either (1) move over and cut the ball off after it bounces and before it hits the side wall, or (2) let it come off the side wall. If you hesitate against the perfect "Z," the ball may get too tight into the back corner or along the back wall and prevent you from taking a good swing.

● If the "Z" has been hit at the proper angle into the front wall, but too low, it will carom off the side wall and come in short of the back wall. So move over, let the ball kick off the side wall, then be ready to go for an offensive return.

● If the "Z" is long, it will carom off the side wall and back wall, then come to you as an offensive setup. Just make sure you're ready to go for the winner off this shot.

Covering Lob Serves

You'll be seeing a lot of lob serves in today's game, even against power hitters, since so many low-drive first serves land short. Therefore, get your ceiling game in precise shape. If your opponent's lob is accurate, just move to the corner and take the ball up to the ceiling as it approaches the back wall. If he's inaccurate, take advantage of your scoring opportunities off the walls. You may be tempted to move up and short-hop the half-lob attempt, but remember: this is a difficult shot to execute under pressure and you lose the point if your racquet travels into the imaginary 5-foot zone too soon.

RELOCATING AFTER YOUR RETURN

If you return the ball offensively, move quickly to the best coverage position you can reach, depending upon where your shot is traveling and where your opponent sets up for his shot. If you hit a ceiling return, simply stay back

COVERING THE "Z" SERVE

The numbers indicate where a properly hit "Z" serve should take its first and second bounces if the defender lets the shot run its course.

When the returner reads an excellent "Z" serve as it comes out of the front right corner (one hit with velocity and at the correct angle), he should quickly move over and contact the ball before it goes into the side wall. Hesitating here and allowing the ball to get into the back corner can lead to an extremely difficult return. Advanced players with good anticipation have the ability to move to the left wall and hit this return offensively.

The defender lets the ball carom off the side wall before making contact, generally going to the ceiling with his return.

A hard "Z," hit perfectly, can angle sharply off the side wall and jam the returner tight against the back wall. Here he's trying to flick out the best possible return in a tough situation.

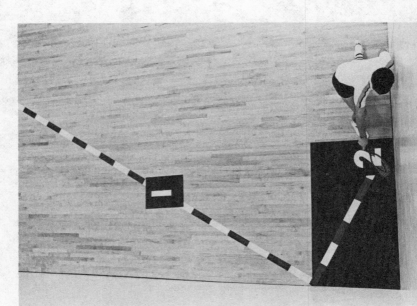

CUTTING OFF THE HALF-LOB

A difficult way to keep from getting caught up in a slower style of play is to move up and contact the half-lob before it carries deep and forces a ceiling return. You can do this by either short-hopping the ball or hitting it on the rise.

The returner moves forward to cut the ball off in the air, but his racquet breaks the imaginary plane 5 feet behind the service box *(left)*. This is illegal by some of today's rules, and the point is awarded to his opponent.

Here, the defender lets the ball bounce but hits it on the rise *(right)*, going for a kill-pass either down-the-wall or cross-court.

and slide off to the side, allowing your opponent to come back and hit. Then adjust accordingly as you see his intentions. (See Chapter 7 for a description of the ceiling-ball rally.)

SERVE RETURN STRATEGY

In developing an overall strategy for your serve return, keep the following concepts in mind, but when you're actually playing, try to think only about flowing with the serve and trusting your instincts.

1. Before each serve, your mental approach should be that first you're looking for the chance to hit an offensive return, and when that opportunity isn't there you'll use common sense and go to the ceiling.

2. Your opponent should always feel the pressure of knowing that if he fails to execute an accurate serve, you have the skills and the confidence to go for an aggressive return to gain an immediate side-out. *You can't become an advanced player if you're scared to shoot the ball at the appropriate time.* If the serve comes into an area where you can take the offensive, you should be going for kill winners or passing shots. Even if a few of these balls angle into the middle of the court at your opponent, he may not have the necessary efficiency to rekill the ball.

3. However, if you realize that you're leaving up too many shots when you try to be aggressive and your opponent is cutting the ball off for winners, or setting up for too many easy scoring shots, then change your strategy: pop the ball to the ceiling more often and wait for more opportune times to be offensive on your return.

4. Also, don't get caught up in your offensive thinking to the point where you take foolish chances against well-executed serves—low-drives, "Z's," and lobs alike—by shoot-

ing every ball. Understand reality and hit the most logical shot: a ceiling ball. Against good players, you can't afford to gamble and consistently leave up your offensive returns in the action zone. Even if you mis-hit your ceiling ball and give your opponent a setup, he's still usually in the back 3 or 4 feet of the court and at least you can move up to cover his offensive attempt.

5.   Remember to mix up your returns. Don't allow the server to lag deep because you're always passing the ball, or to stay close to the service box because you try to pinch every return.

IMPROVING YOUR RETURN

Here are some different approaches:

First, evaluate just how effectively you're presently returning the ball under match-play pressure. When a friend is charting one of your matches, have him watch to see if your offensive returns are hitting low enough into the front wall to either go for winners, jam your opponent in center court, or go by him for effective passing shots. How well are you angling the ball away from him with pinches and passes? By comparison, how often do you leave the ball up and give him scoring opportunities? When you go to the ceiling, do you dictate another ceiling shot—or simply give him a setup?

Second, when practicing with a friend, make sure you take a variety of serves to your forehand side so you're accustomed to reading the ball into that corner and executing from there while on the move or stretched out.

Third, help improve your judgment and reflexes against the "Z" by having a friend hit "Z's" to you for 5 minutes while you call out "good," "short," or "long" before the ball reaches the short line. Also, when watching other matches study where the "Z" tends to travel after hitting into the front corner at different heights and angles—and how the "Z" pattern changes according to where the ball hits on the front wall.

Fourth, expand your capabilities against low-drives deep into the corners so that (1) you can return more shots more effectively to the ceiling, and (2) you can begin to hit offensive returns against serves that are not perfect, but which fail to come off the walls as setups. Since you have little time to get your racquet on the ball, concentrate on mastering that quick, fluid movement toward the side wall—starting with the cross-over step—so you're in a position to cut off some of your opponent's low-drives and take them low zone. At first, practice this complete movement without the ball coming to you. Then, starting from your normal ready position, throw a ball over into the corner and go after it, hitting offensively and defensively as you are stretching out. Finally, work on this total unit as a friend hits low-drives into both corners.

Fifth, in practice matches try to go for the offensive return when you normally might opt for the ceiling return, especially under tournament pressure. Also try to put the ball away instead of always using safer passing shots. Not that you turn the match into a circus by trying to shoot every return, skipping most of them and alienating your opponent, who wants to get into good racquetball rallies. Just stretch yourself a bit to see how effective you can be with a more offensive approach and to gain greater confidence in these shots. You're eventually going to need them to keep moving up the racquetball ladder.

CHAPTER 7

SHOTS FOR AN ALL-AROUND GAME

In building a solid game that enables you to play offensively and defensively, your arsenal should eventually include a variety of basic shots—from pinches and passes to ceilings and overheads. When you can hit these shots with control and confidence, you strengthen your play in four ways:

1. You force your opponent to have the ability to cover all areas of the court.
2. You are able to capitalize on his weaknesses.
3. He must play you honest in his positioning.
4. You can hang in there longer in many more rallies.

This chapter will detail how you can improve your accuracy with these shots and how to use them effectively. Chapter 10 will discuss how to integrate them into a sound strategy of shot selection.

PASSING SHOTS

Actually, there are two kinds of passes that occur in advanced racquetball today. The first is a kill-pass attempt where you're going for the straight-in kill or cross-court, but you'll settle for a winner that goes past your opponent down-the-line or cross-court. Second is the planned passing shot, which is hit not with a kill shot in mind but to drive an opponent out of good coverage position and force a weak return. I feel this is an undeveloped shot and a weak link for many advancing players, especially those who have become overly enamored with the kill attempt.

If you want to be offensive but you're not sufficiently set up for a kill attempt, recognize the quiet virtues of *planned passing shots*, cross-court and down-the-line. Certainly you flirt with danger as you try to hit your proper front-wall passing targets from varying locations on the court: misangled shots travel directly into the middle of the court or carom off a side wall, and since you're deliberately aiming a little higher, it's difficult to keep the ball off the back wall. However, you can't afford to slight the intentioned pass—particularly a down-the-liner—as you work to diversify your game. Rallies everywhere are dominated by cross-court shots of varying heights and angles, possibly because everyone feels safer hitting toward the middle of the front wall where the margin for error seems much greater. Yet when your opponent must respect your down-the-line ability, he can't afford to overplay your cross-court angle.

THE PINCH SHOT

Simply put, you need a reliable pinch shot into both front corners because of the crucial dimension it gives your game: *an important scoring shot that forces your opponent to respect the front part of the court.*

When you avoid the pinch shot by continually passing the ball or going for the straight-in kill, a competent opponent will feel comfortable lagging back as you shoot. He doesn't have to fear your pinches and he knows that your

Hitting from the right side of the court, this player has two good passing angles to force his opponent out of center court. Both shots should take their first bounce on or before the "1" areas shown on the court, in order to keep the ball off the back wall.

Since the defender is playing close to the back service line, making him more capable of digging up potential winners and cutting off regular cross-court passes, the hitter smartly widens his angle to drive the ball around his opponent for a winner.

left-up kills and misangled passes will funnel into his hittable area. However, when he knows you can pinch the ball for winners, he must constantly worry about being ready to thrust forward to dig up your slight "misses" in and around the service box area. Even when he does get his racquet on the ball, he very often gives you a setup for another scoring opportunity.

There are three basic types of pinches, as shown in the photos:

1. The best pinch is hit *tightly into the corner*, catching the nearest side wall within several feet of the front wall and less than 12 inches high (or low enough to make the ball bounce twice before the service box or the opposite side wall). A tight pinch that goes front wall-side wall can be equally effective when kept low, but will always angle directly to your opponent when hit too high.

2. The *wide-angle pinch*, which strikes farther back on the side wall and then contacts the front wall near the middle, is also a valuable shot but much more difficult to master. You can use it to angle the ball away from your opponent, forcing him to the side of the court, but it's hard to make the ball bounce twice for a winner before it kicks off the opposite side wall.

3. At higher levels of play, you'll find yourself needing *a reverse pinch*, which is aimed tight into the opposite side-wall corner and can be hit at varying distances from the side wall. This pinch travels away from your opponent and forces him diagonally forward into a difficult coverage position, but beware: leave the ball up and you give him an easy setup.

The pinch is an integral part of advanced play and should be approached aggressively as a kill-shot opportunity that can't be avoided. Although you're deliberately using the side wall, which can send the ball right back to your opponent if you error to the high side, you are also

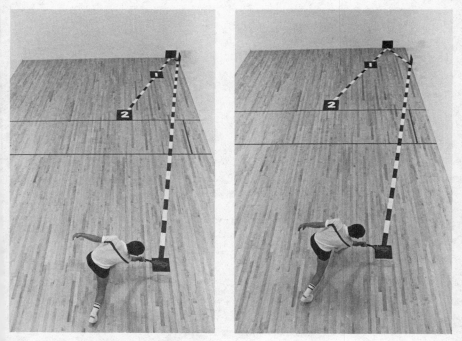

THE REGULAR PINCH SHOT

Notice in these pictures, as the hitter pinches the ball from about 30 feet, how the angle changes as he hits farther back on the side wall and where the second bounce occurs. Strive to hit all these pinches a foot or lower on the side wall, even when you are aiming 10 or 15 feet from the front wall. The wide-angle pinch in the last photo (p. 112) may look easy to hit, but find out for yourself how difficult it is to make the ball bounce twice before the opposite side wall. Experiment by yourself with different angles from different positions on the court so you become aware of the exact patterns of the pinch. For example, try the pinch shown here from about 5 feet to the left and see how all these angles change.

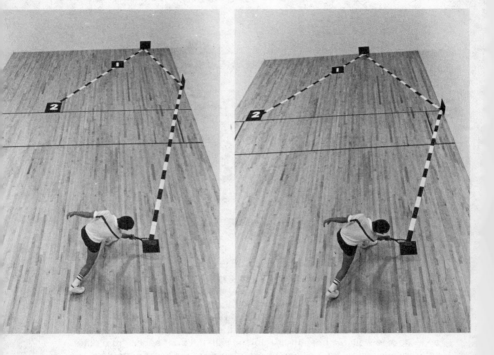

The front-wall–side-wall pinch is an important *planned* shot that diversifies your attack. However, in fast-action exchanges, it's also a shot that's going to happen by accident as you try to hit a tight pinch off the side wall, or go down-the-wall. One advantage of this pinch is that you may catch your opponent moving in the wrong direction as he anticipates a down-the-line pass or a regular pinch.

forcing him to move up by angling the ball low and away, from where he's positioned.

Hit the pinch hard, but also learn how and when to take some pace off the shot—without trying to "dink" the ball—so it has a greater chance of taking two bounces close to the front wall. As another advanced technique to maximize your effectiveness, also work on hitting the ball with overspin when you drive the ball into the side wall. I find that this is the only way I can consistently keep my pinches traveling low as they come off the front wall.

The "Splat"

This is a hard-velocity pinch shot, contacted very close to the side wall, which has an excessive amount of spin and

THE REVERSE PINCH

Advanced players are becoming increasingly competent with this shot (for example, by using the left wall for a forehand pinch, instead of the right wall). The numbers on the court in these pictures indicate where the ball will usually take its first and second bounce when pinched hard, about 12 inches high along the side wall. In the final picture, the player is hitting the wall too far back, making it virtually impossible for the ball to bounce twice before the opposite side wall. This shot almost always caroms back toward center court for a setup.

reacts unpredictably off the front wall. You hit the ball with the same stroke that you use going down-the-line, but when you give it a glancing blow off the side wall, it picks up English and can react in a number of ways. When hit properly it may (1) spin sharply off the front wall like a perfect pinch, or (2) streak down the middle of the court as a difficult shot to cut off and put away, or (3) spin off the front wall and actually angle by your opponent for a perfect cross-court pass.

The splat has emerged in recent years, benefiting many of the power hitters, and it may evolve as an advanced specialty shot in your own game—once you master a solid power swing. If you do, use it sparingly, for it remains at best a feast-or-famine type of shot: great when it reacts in your favor, but one that, because of the angle used, can often come back into center-court as an easy setup.

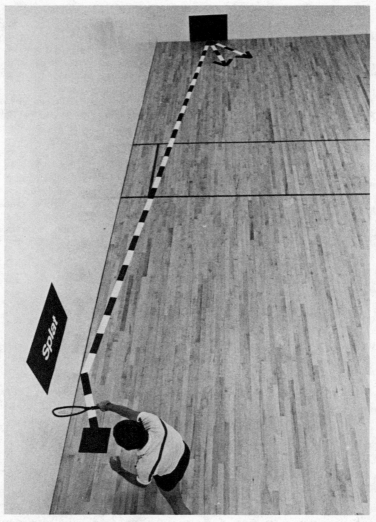

The "splat" is driven hard into the side wall—from chest high and below—
imparting considerable spin and English on the ball, which can cause it to
squirt off the front wall in an unpredictable direction.

This shot should only be attempted when you're contacting the ball less than 2 feet from a side wall (and even then a smarter percentage play is the straight-in kill or a passing shot); trying for the splat effect any farther away requires an extremely powerful stroke. Several top players feel that the splat is also an excellent way to be offensive with the ball from shoulder level, but again, you have to really drive the ball hard into the side wall—with the correct angle—to make it work.

The Modified Down-the-Line

Another shot that often occurs in top play is the modified down-the-line. When this shot is hit from deep court, very near the side wall, the ball contacts the wall at about the service box area and can then react in one of several ways as it comes off the front wall. When hit very low, it has a knuckle-ball effect, squirting back in to the side wall and going for a winner in front court. Hit higher, it angles back down the line for a perfect pass. However, when this shot is slightly mis-hit, the ball can easily angle into center-court for a plum. (Experiment on an empty court and see how this shot reacts off the side and front walls.)

The nature of this shot is such that you should take it when it occurs and not necessarily preplan it. For example, it occurs many times off a planned down-the-line shot that is slightly misangled.

THE CEILING BALL

If your goal is a flexible style of play—where you can retrieve effectively, change the pace of the rally when necessary, and cope with the blaster as well as the junker—*you must develop a reliable ceiling-ball shot off the forehand and backhand sides.* Very often we underestimate the ceil-

The modified down-the-line hits the side wall closer to the front wall than a splat. After striking the front wall, the ball will either carom back into the side wall or travel closely down the wall for a pass.

ing ball's importance, viewing it as a boring interloper in the power game. Yet in many ways it has a crucial influence at every level of play. For example:

● The ceiling ball is the best defensive shot against your opponent's tough, well-angled serves (lobs as well as low-drives and "Z's").

● It's your best percentage response to an opponent's well-placed ceiling ball.

● It's almost always your smartest defensive shot when your opponent goes low zone and you can barely get your racquet on the ball and you need to get a toehold in the rally. Even if your ceiling comes in short and gives your opponent a setup, the ceiling ball stymies his offensive assault for a moment, forcing him deep and giving you time to gain a good coverage position.

● If your opponent has an erratic ceiling ball, you may want to go to the ceiling with offense in the back of your mind: when you force him to the back of the court, his return (either a ceiling or a lower-percentage overhead) may give you a low-zone opportunity.

● The ceiling can also be used as a tactical weapon to change the tempo of a rally, forcing your oponent to shift gears, which may draw some errors when you get him out of a low-zone groove.

If you can hit the ball harder than anybody in your club, it's a big mistake to scoff at the idea of mastering a ceiling-ball game. Even in a match between power players such as Marty Hogan and Dave Peck there are many ceiling balls and often long ceiling-ball rallies, because they've learned the importance of that shot and how to hit it with touch and control. The reason all top players get locked into lengthy ceiling-ball exchanges is that neither player wants to take a low-percentage kill attempt, for fear he'll leave the shot up for his opponent to re-kill. Thus, each player is waiting out his opponent, hoping for a mis-hit ceiling ball that will give him a better scoring opportunity.

Stroking Technique

Depending upon the ball being used (slow or live), adjust your ceiling targets and the force of your stroke accordingly.

When playing with a slow (pressureless) ball, aim for a target area about 3 feet before the front wall. Hit the ball with enough force so that it caroms down to the floor, then travels in a high arc and strikes the back wall no higher than 2 feet. This desired arc dictates another ceiling or an overhead drive attempt and your opponent is rarely going to hurt you offensively. Try to aim for the same ceiling target when playing with a lively (pressurized) ball, but "feather" it up there with a light touch. If necessary, move your target back from the front wall, but still take pace off the ball. The live ball is certainly harder to control as you strive to keep it from rebounding off the back wall as a setup, but through practice you'll become comfortable at maintaining a soft touch on the ball.

When working on the ceiling ball, remember these checkpoints:

● Practice with a variety of balls so you become familiar with their characteristics and what it takes to have each ball carry low into the back wall.

● Your stroke is going to be adaptable, in relation to how high you actually contact the ball, so make sure you hit along both walls against balls that come to you at different heights (a drill you can easily do on your own).

● On the forehand side, your basic motion is like throwing a ball over a high fence. Just concentrate on getting that desired shoulder action into the shot and the feel of that motion coming through as you hit dozens of balls; then you can begin worrying about how high the ball is

THE FOREHAND CEILING BALL

Most players find that it's easier to "feather" the ball up to the ceiling by hitting from an open stance, with the feet planted. The hitting motion is brief—this is the furthest back I draw my racquet—and my left arm is kept in to provide balance.

THE BACKHAND CEILING BALL

When going to the ceiling from the backhand side, you'll often find it more natural to swing from a closed stance. Notice how the racquet is pulled back and the shoulders are turned, enabling me to use my upper body as I pull through the shot with a smooth controlled stroke.

hitting on the back wall. When going to the ceiling against lower balls, use a side-arm type swing.

● On backhands, once you learn to pull through with the hitting shoulder, you can use this same motion against any ball that comes to you from knee to shoulder level. (You may find it helpful to get in front of a mirror and compare your stroke to the accompanying photographs.)

● Complete your swing off both sides and avoid an abrupt ending; let the racquet arm flow through so you maintain a rhythmical motion. Just as in golf, you want to *swing* at the ball and let it take its natural course; don't try to consciously aim it or guide it or poke it up to the ceiling.

● Top players are applying English to their forehand when they have a chance to slightly cut across the ball at impact. This tends to take a little power off the shot and helps provide slightly better control, but the shot can be hit equally well by coming straight through the ball.

Placement and Relocation

Ideally, unless you're going cross-court, try to have your ceiling shot hug a side wall to give your opponent a more difficult return—but *keep the ball off the wall,* or you'll risk giving him a plum setup. Error toward the middle of the court, and short of the back wall, since players today are fully capable of hitting winners off long ceiling balls. In practice, also work on hitting cross-court into both back corners with both strokes (alone, or with a friend as you exchange ceiling balls). Then, under pressure, you'll begin to feel comfortable going to an opponent's backhand from any part of the court, whether he's a righty or a lefty.

(As you work on this shot, try to have a friend watch where your ball hits the ceiling so you can concentrate on your stroke and where the ball ends up. If your shots are constantly falling short—using a slower ball—the problem may not be your stroke or how hard you're swinging; very likely, the ball is striking the ceiling too far back and the

When practicing alone, let your ceiling balls pass by and see how often they hit about 2 feet high on the back wall. This is your ideal target area, since it forces your opponent to contact the ball at about shoulder level.

subsequent angle makes it virtually impossible for the ball to travel deep enough.)

When you see that you've hit a good ceiling shot, remember: it's going to push your opponent deep and generally dictate another ceiling, so save your energy by staying back. Move aside laterally as you watch him go to hit, then either wait for the ball to come back to you if it's another ceiling, or move to cover either an overhead attempt or around-the-wall ball. Of course, if you see that your ceiling is going to give your opponent a scoring opportunity, move up and hope that he leaves his shot up.

THE OVERHEAD

Even if you have an excellent ceiling shot, the overhead drive—used judiciously—can enable you to play a more versatile, aggressive game.

First of all, the overhead should be viewed primarily as a combination shot to set yourself up for a better scoring opportunity, not as an all-or-nothing winner (which is a rarity even in the pro game). An overhead passing shot, low and away from your opponent, can force him to hit while on the move or stretched out, thus increasing your chances of getting a weak return.

Second, a controlled overhead gives you flexibility against an opponent's ceiling balls and high-lob "Z" serves that are only slightly mis-hit. You can step up and take the ball down low, instead of automatically going up to the ceiling because you fear the efficiency of your overhead.

Third, you can initiate a low-zone type rally even against the seemingly perfect ceiling ball or lob-"Z"-type serve. If you have little patience for ceiling-ball rallies—and perhaps a weak ceiling shot—the overhead can force your opponent to play a faster-paced game more to your liking.

Having taken this stand for the overhead's *potential*

THE OVERHEAD

The overhead drive, generally hit off a short ceiling ball, is aimed into the front wall as a passing shot away from your opponent—and low enough to stay off the back wall as a setup.

The overhead kill is pinched low and tight into the opposite front corner, a difficult feat (and an unreasonable expectation) when you're trying to bring the ball down from above your head, low enough to bounce twice before the service box.

virtues, I must stress its definite drawback: you're hitting down at such an angle that it takes great accuracy to make the ball bounce twice before the back wall. Moreover, when you're deep and you leave the overhead up off the back wall, your opponent can easily move over and be offensive with his shot as you scramble for a coverage position.

The Overhead Kill

Trying to deliberately end the rally with an overhead kill is such a risky, sometimes foolhardy ploy that you should attempt it only infrequently—when you have a high-bouncing setup well short of the back wall, and especially if your opponent is caught deep. If he knows you have some skill with this shot and that you're not afraid to gamble at an opportune time, then he can't afford to always lag deep when you set up for an overhead. Give him something to think about, but remember: this is still a low-percentage shot, and very seldom can you beat opponents of equal ability with low-percentage shots. I also find that a player's overhead efficiency tends to go down as he gets closer to game point. He may feel comfortable going for the kill at 5-all, but his execution seems to suffer when the pressure's on at 18-all.

In going for the overhead kill, try to pinch the ball tightly into either corner and hope that it bounces twice before your opponent can get up to cover it.

SHOTS OFF THE BACK WALL

Taking the ball off the back wall should be one of your easiest and most reliable scoring shots, since you're setting up on a ball that's dropping low and is already headed for the front wall. However, if you realize that you're less efficient with this shot than many of your opponents, or that you're not putting it away as consistently as you want, here are some key fundamentals to review:

1. Go back with the single purpose of shooting the ball, even from 35 to 36 feet. The better players today are always thinking offensively when they retreat for this shot, even against a cross-court pass that is going to travel deep, nick the side wall, and barely come off the back wall. You may be happy just to get a shot like this back up to the front wall, but your tougher opponents, in the same situation, may be thinking, "If the ball comes off the back wall just enough to give me room to swing, I'm going to score."

2. The key to this shot is your movement with the ball, so don't get lazy. Make sure you're getting back quickly, and close enough to the back wall, so that you can come out with the ball as it rebounds forward.

3. As you move out with the ball, have your racquet in its set position and use whatever footwork style is comfortable. Let the ball drop low to your power zone as you stride in, then take a whipping jai-alai-type stroke, striving to have your body going totally into the shot at impact.

4. In practice, hit a variety of shots off the back wall and work on your movement so that you feel confident and competent in a match. Also diversify your low-zone shots, mixing up pinches, straight-in kills, and passes to keep opponents from playing off your tendencies.

THE AROUND-THE-WALL BALL

This is a shot you should incorporate into your game as an occasionally useful alternative to the ceiling—either to throw a different hitting angle at your opponent or to recover defensively.

A good around-the-wall ball (ARWB) is directed high

SHOTS OFF THE BACK WALL

The player is retreating with the ball as it heads for the back wall, and he's anticipating how far it will carry out.

He wants to be far enough back so that he can move out with the ball as he sets up in a power-hitting position. He must shoot a variety of kill attempts from this area to keep his opponent from anticipating a particular shot.

and with moderate speed into a side wall, so that it carries across the court and strikes the opposite side wall above the service box. The ball is still in the air as it then caroms diagonally across the court, while slanting downward. If your opponent is aggressive and has a solid stroke, he should be able to fly-kill the ball before it bounces. However, this shot is tougher to put away than it looks, especially if your opponent has ignored it in practice and is now trying to execute under pressure, knowing that you're ready to cover any miss. Also, if he's grooved into returning ceiling balls, he's familiar with that ball pattern and he may now error as he tries to hit a ball that's coming diagonally off a side wall. Of course, he can let the ball bounce and then take it up to the ceiling, but here again he's contacting the ball at an unfamiliar angle.

I also use the around-the-wall ball when I'm stretched out of position and I need to buy time to get back in the rally. This is an automatic decision when I feel I don't have a good angle to flip it to the ceiling, so I drive it up into the side wall.

THE "Z" BALL

You're not going to fool anybody in advanced play with the "Z" ball, but you may find it useful as a tactic to either change pace or to retrieve when you're unable to hit a ceiling or an around-the-wall ball.

The "Z" ball resembles the around-the-wall ball, except that it hits the front wall first and then the side wall before caroming to the opposite side wall in the back 10 feet of the court. This pattern can confuse a novice, but the experienced player simply drifts over and, depending on how well the shot has been hit, either goes defensively to the ceiling or sets up for an offensive shot as the ball rebounds off the side wall and/or back wall.

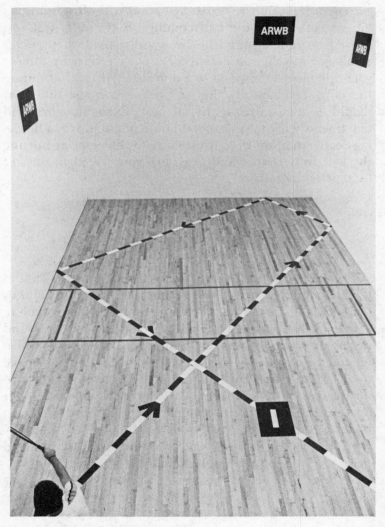

THE AROUND-THE-WALL BALL

This particular around-the-wall ball strikes the right wall quite high, then traces a path shown in the photograph, hitting the left wall about 10 to 12 feet high and taking its first bounce near the middle of the court. It will carom into the side wall and then angle toward the back wall, ideally not coming off as a setup.

You can pick up an occasional point with this shot if it's hit perfectly, with the ball coming off the side wall and getting in tight against the back wall. Also, when things aren't going well, you may draw a weak return by forcing your opponent to respond to a different type of shot during the rally. Yet basically the "Z" ball is a fringe shot that should be used infrequently, at best. Even though it will buy time when you're desperate on defense, this is a lingering-death situation if your opponent is efficient at putting the ball away from deep court and your "Z" ball doesn't have perfect accuracy.

HITTING INTO THE BACK WALL

In the course of a rally, when your opponent's shot is threatening to get past you deep in the court, hitting into the back wall should be a last-resort option. Unless you're able to really drive the ball hard, this shot tends to rebound weakly off the front wall, enabling your opponent to move up and go for the fly-kill. Of course, when you can make the back wall shot carry high into the front wall with reasonable velocity, it will at least carry back and force your opponent to set up from beyond 30 feet. Given the choice, however, I try to flick my desperate retrieving shots directly up to the ceiling or front wall because it's a little easier to make the ball go high and rebound deep.

CHAPTER 8

CUTTING THE BALL OFF

When your opponent's offensive attempt has been left up and is coming hard through the heart of the action zone, you must know how and when to cut this shot off, in the air or after one bounce. Even though the ball will come off the back wall if you let it go by, there are going to be many times in a match when you should capitalize on the situation by intercepting the ball and taking it back down low to score. You can't back off, for this aggressiveness—just like volleying at the net in tennis—will give your game a boost in several important ways.

First, you'll score more easy points as you take advantage of your positioning in the center-court area. Instead of moving back to play the ball off the back wall—and giving your opponent a chance to move forward into a prime coverage position—you can end the point quickly with a straight-in kill, a tight pinch, or a pass. Even if you leave the ball up, you're still in good court position to cover your opponent's next shot.

Second, by holding your position and forcing the action, you'll keep a toehold in the center court—where you want to be. You'll also reduce your opponent's offensive potential and draw many weak returns by keeping him constantly on the move and under considerable pressure.

Third, if your opponent is off-balance or out of position after hitting, you'll have a variety of scoring options and it will be easier for you to angle the ball away from him—as a pinch or a pass—before he can recover. In addition, you can use your body positioning to legally block him off as you snap the ball into the open court area.

When you shy away from cut-off opportunities by letting every possible ball carry into the back wall, you must fight uphill against an aggressive opponent who understands the importance of controlling center court. Every time you go back to set up in deep court, he'll be moving forward into a prime coverage position and the pressure will now be on you to hit a perfect kill or pass to score points. You may be ripping for winners, but if you miss just a little he's going to be able to cover nearly all of these shots—and most of them from up ahead of you. In short, he's going to control the match.

STRATEGY DECISIONS

Through experience and practice, you'll gain the instincts needed to quickly judge whether you should cut the ball off or let it go through to the back wall. A useful guideline has always been: hold your ground against all balls that are coming to you *at waist level or below*. True, this is the kind of decision that must be made at advanced levels, but it's not always hard-and-fast. For example:

● If the ball is scorching through the center-court at about waist level and you know that you're going to be forcing an offensive shot by trying to cut it off, it will be wiser to let the ball rebound off the back wall, enabling you to set up for a higher-percentage kill attempt.

CUTTING THE BALL OFF

When cutting the ball off, you're often forced to hit from an open stance, with your body virtually facing the front wall, and without stepping into the ball. Here's where you need a sound upper-body swing and hip rotation.

Top players learn to strike the ball when it's only a foot off the floor.

All advanced players must be able to hit the ball offensively when it's coming in at around knee height.

This is a crucial area that needs regular attention in practice. Instead of always letting a shot like this carry off the back wall, work on cutting it off efficiently at about waist level, especially when your opponent is out of position, or on your left hip and you want to kill it or drive it away from him for an immediate winner.

Bringing the ball down low from around chest level takes a high degree of skill, but this offensive approach can put great pressure on an opponent who's out of position and trying to scramble back into play. Remember, however, that this shot will easily carom off the back wall, so use good discretion when cutting a ball off this way.

● If your opponent is already well-positioned—and you're scrambling or off-balance—instinct may tell you to take your chances by letting the ball go past.

● If you realize that you're simply keeping the ball in play or giving your opponent setups, then be less aggressive here as you play important matches—but work hard on your technique in practice so that you can begin hitting the ball really low and accurately into the corners and the front wall.

When cutting the ball off, maintaining your position is not enough; you must be thinking low zone, going for outright winners or shots that at least keep pressure on your opponent by forcing him forward or to the side. If you fail to really do anything with the ball except rehit it, then eventually you're going to give your opponent a shot he can put away. (I see this problem occurring with players who try to play too close to the service box. Although they may cut many balls off, very often they only have time to punch a shot harmlessly into the front wall. By moving back 3 or 4 feet as their opponent sets up to hit, they would gain enough reaction time to put away a few balls and end some rallies in their favor.)

TECHNIQUE AND IMPROVEMENT

Cutting the ball off properly is a difficult skill to acquire and one that demands constant attention in terms of your reactions, movements to the ball, racquet control, and execution.

Since you're contacting the ball at different angles as it comes to you, usually waist high or below, you must rely on adaptable form (which is discussed in Chapter 4). As stressed there, concentrate on giving yourself as much time as possible to get your body into a solid but efficient hitting position—ideally, with your feet planted firmly, since you'll

When cutting the ball off in center court, the hitter wants to be thinking "low zone"—the entire area from the corners across the front wall—but he can actually score with 5 types of shots: pinches into either corner, kill-pass attempts, or the straight-in kill.

The hitter is positioned for a definite scoring opportunity. Although her opponent is already moving to the right in anticipation, her best shot is a down-the-wall kill or pass. However, she should also mix in tight pinch shots to keep her opponent "honest."

not have time to actually step into the ball. Carry your racquet around midthigh so you're ready to set up quickly and you're free to rotate your upper body into the shot, pulling through with a full but compact follow-through. Use your legs and hips as much as time allows and strive for solid contact with the ball, putting direction and accuracy ahead of power. Racquet control is also important because sometimes you'll want to drive a passing shot down-the-wall when your opponent is out of position, sometimes you'll try to take off a little speed as you block the ball into the corner, and other times you'll want to pinch the ball hard with overspin.

Learning to do all this confidently, under pressure, requires concentrated practice sessions. Yet here's a simple drill that will enable you to work on all the basic principles, alone or with a friend. Stand about 25 to 27 feet from the front wall in the middle of the court and start rallying by yourself (or with your friend), holding your position and cutting off as many balls as you can that come to you around waist high or below. At first, simply concentrate on hitting off your forehand side, driving the ball low into the front wall; if it comes back to you on two bounces, still try to make a play. Eventually, however, cover both sides of the court and consciously try for pinches, passes, and straight-in kills.

THE LOW-ZONE RALLY

Your ability to cut the ball off is going to prove crucial in low-zone rallies, where you and your opponent are suddenly caught up trying to put the ball away while scrambling to hold your ground in the center-court area. In these intense, close-quarter exchanges, where there's little time to swing with picture-perfect form, you'll both be hitting the ball low—but not low enough or accurately enough to win the point outright. Thus, you'll be hitting from an open stance one moment—reacting to a ball coming straight at you—and an instant later you may be stretching out and digging up your opponent's potential winner. Here's where you must have the ability to adjust quickly and move into a position to take a quick, solid stroke as often as possible, so that you can make that difficult volley or the "reflex" shot where you don't have time to think. By hanging in the rally like this and keeping your opponent moving and off-balance, you'll find yourself winning more than your share of points.

Here again, rally against yourself from around 23 to 30 feet, trying to return every ball that comes to you about waist high or below. This will probably exhaust you in 5 minutes, but you'll be forced to take all the different strokes that come up in a quick-reaction rally—against balls that rebound directly off the front wall or carom off a side wall.

CHAPTER 9

COVERING YOUR OPPONENT'S SHOTS

After you hit the ball, you can't control what happens next, yet you can certainly improve your odds by (1) being in the best possible coverage position as your opponent goes to shoot, and (2) moving quickly and efficiently to the ball. Your opponent may be hitting the right shot, but if you're positioned properly—by having studied his stroke, anticipating his shot selection, and knowing his capabilities—you'll make it much more difficult for him to score points. You'll also make it easier for yourself to reach more balls and to hit more shots from good positions. This in turn helps keep your opponent on the defensive and more likely to give you weaker returns—if you're executing.

Obviously, you're going to find it easier to effectively cover more of the court by having an agile body and strong legs. Yet you can certainly compensate here by using your head when you play and mastering the subtleties of court coverage.

KEY FACTORS IN POSITIONING

Unless you're in a ceiling-ball rally, your prime coverage position for an opponent's particular shot should fluctuate in relation to the following factors (and change subtly as the match progresses and you learn more about your opponent):

- the type of shot you've hit
- where your opponent will be hitting
- what type of shot he is likely going to attempt
- his capabilities and tendencies with that shot.

Top players know they can't afford to get locked in to one prime position whenever their opponent is going low zone. So they try to cover as many shots as possible from a position that floats from about 22 feet back to nearly 30 feet, and is about midway between the side walls—but shaded slightly to their opponent's side (unless they are "cheating" by anticipating a predictable shot). When driven out of this zone by their opponent's shot, they fight to get back in after hitting. And when they hit a misdirected shot that forces them to move aside and open up hitting lanes for their opponent, they hone back in the moment the ball passes.

Adjusting to Your Opponent's Ability

As you watch your opponent move to the ball, play off his likely hitting position, but also try to sense: will your shot give him an offensive opportunity and, if so, what is his scoring potential from this particular spot on the court? For example, if you've driven him deep with a passing shot and he's going to be hitting while on the move, you can usually lag back at around 28 to 30 feet and play the percentages: if he tries to go low zone, his chances of killing the ball are slim and his shot is much more likely to rebound back into your hitting zone. However, if he's hitting from about that same area on the court, but setting up on a ball that's going to carom off the side wall—and he has a much greater chance of killing this ball—you'll want to migrate up about a stride. From this position you can cover any shot that comes within your range, but you're especially ready to thrust forward to either re-kill or dig up his potential winner. (The photographs in this chapter show typical coverage situations that will arise in every match.)

Against a new opponent, try positioning yourself at around 25 feet when you've given him an obvious setup. *Make him prove that he can indeed kill the ball—consistently in front of you.* If he can, fine. You'll be forced to hold your position and be alert in your court coverage. But if he's leaving all his shots up, learn to lag back a bit more and adjust your positions accordingly. Don't let a fear of your opponent's potential kill shots lure you too far forward as he goes to hit. Remember: you'll rarely reach a ball that bounces twice inside of 15 feet and you'll leave yourself vulnerable to being easily passed or jammed the closer you are to the back service line. *More of your opponent's kill attempts are going to be coming back deeper than you think, so stay back a bit, ready to cover those misses.* When a smart opponent sees that you like to hug the short line, he can simply adjust his shot selection and continually direct the ball around you with wide-angled passing shots. You also give him the confidence that he doesn't have to hit an effective kill in the front 15 feet to win the point, thus taking pressure off him and putting it back on yourself to cover all of his shots.

Playing Off Your Opponent's Tendencies

When playing a person for the first time, cover his shots straight up until you begin to sense his shot-making tendencies as well as his abilities. All players have preferences when hitting offensively from specific areas on the court, but many fall into a comfortable and predictable pattern of shot selection. If you're alert, this lack of diversification can allow you to overplay one side of the court, or to move up or lag back as he goes to hit. On a court where a foot or two difference in any direction has a critical influence, this extra edge in covering your opponent's offensive shots

Many hitters tend to pinch the ball off the side wall or drive it cross-court when going low zone from fairly deep along the side wall *(left)*. Therefore, the defender here is studying his opponent's swing and is ready to cover off to his right (as the arrows indicate) to capitalize on this predictability. Anticipation like this can make it difficult for the hitter to execute successful offensive shots.

Most players, when they get into pressure situations, tend to hit the same type of shot from a particular area on the court *(right)*. If the hitter here always tries for the same cross-court angle in key situations, the defender should "feel" that tendency and be ready to move directly to the left side of the court to minimize this shot's effectiveness.

places greater pressure on him to execute. Play off these tendencies until he begins to prove you wrong—not with one great shot that catches you flat-footed or moving the wrong way, but a number of good shots.

Here are several common examples of positioning strategies:

● If your opponent sets up on the forehand side and always tries to either pinch into the right corner or go cross-court, shade to the left of center, since the ball is heading here if he leaves either shot up. Challenge him to pass you cleanly down the right side.

● If another opponent is aggressive from the forehand side with good down-the-line and cross-court kills and passes, and also possesses a tough pinch, he forces you to play more honestly in your coverage. Here you must position yourself far enough on the right side to respect that 6- or 7-foot alley down the right wall—but be equally ready to break left for his cross-court attempt, or to go up for a pinch.

● This same opponent with a versatile forehand may tend to hit every backhand cross-court, in which case you should edge over to the right side and lag a bit until he proves he can hurt you with passes down the left wall or pinches into the left corner.

After playing an opponent several times, you'll start to have a mental book on him when he hits from a particular location on the court. But if he still continually burns you with a certain shot, try to watch his match against another player. See if his shot selection is obvious and how this other opponent adjusts. (It's also easier to notice these patterns when you're not playing.) Meanwhile, when observing potential opponents around the club, look for tendencies in their shot selection that you might anticipate when you play them.

Studying Your Opponent's Swing

Good anticipation starts with your ability to watch the ball and then your opponent's stroke *right up until impact* (or just slightly before). This enables you to look back to the front wall already knowing that he's going to the ceiling or low zone—and you're ready to react accordingly. Advanced players try to camouflage their low-zone intentions by hitting all their offensive shots off the same motion. Yet many of these players fail to hide these intentions as well as they think they do, and by studying how they set up on the ball and their body positioning you can begin to sense what they're going to hit.

If you're hesitant about studying your opponent's swing when he's behind you, fearing you'll get hit in the eye, then wear eyeguards. After a period of adjustment, you should find yourself playing better with them on, since they give you confidence to watch the ball right into your opponent's racquet, free of fears of being badly hurt (which in turn helps you play more aggressively and with greater concentration on the ball). It's true, of course, that most pros fail to wear eyeguards. One reason is that they have confidence in their opponent's accuracy and shot selection; they know they can watch him and not have to fear a wildly inaccurate or out-of-the-blue type of shot. They've also learned through experience when to duck or tuck back in early if they sense a dangerous situation. If you can acquire these instincts and the correct positioning, you should be able to play safely without eyeguards—but I would still recommend the insurance they offer.

MOVING TO THE BALL

Try to keep your body relaxed and fairly erect as you watch your opponent take his swing. Then, if he's going low zone, widen your base slightly as you turn to the front

◄ COVERING THE BALL

The defender is in center court, studying his opponent's stroke and trying to anticipate the shot. Note how he's ready to move quickly in any direction from a solid coverage position: a wide stance, knees bent, and body open to the front wall.

The defender turns back to the front wall slightly before or just at impact, ready to react to the shot.

He moves left with a cross-over step to cover the cross-court pass while his opponent moves into a coverage position.

wall, keeping your knees comfortably bent. You want to remain flexible, in a low, stable position so you're able to move strongly and fluidly to track down a shot that isn't killed or that doesn't come directly at you.

Experience is going to teach you which footwork methods get you to the ball quickly and in control, ready to execute your best possible stroke. From good covering positions, you should be able to move 7 or 8 feet in any direction and reach the majority of your opponent's left-up shots with no more than a stride (or a cross-over step) and a stretch. But to reach those well-angled passes that are tight against a side wall, your serve-return technique is essential: the quick cross-over step, a long stretch, and then a full extension with your hitting arm and racquet.

When analyzing your court movement (on videotape or with the help of a friend), look for unnecessary movements that may be slowing you down and/or wasting excess energy. For example, even some top players have a bad habit of unconsciously jumping up slightly as their opponent hits, instead of getting into a solid position and staying low when they turn to the front wall. This may sound like a trivial problem, but I've found through frame-by-frame videotape analysis that when a player hops up like this (or stands upright instead of getting into a lowered position), his opponent's low-zone shot is practically to the front wall by the time his feet are firmly set to move. The ball is moving so fast that these lost split seconds can make the difference between reaching the ball—and reaching it in time to rip away.

The Value of Retrieving Ability

You can strengthen your game in two important ways when you have a determination to fight for every point and the ability to get your racquet on one apparent winner after another, even if you can only flick the ball to the ceiling or the front wall.

First, by at least keeping the ball in play when you're stretched out to the side or thrusting forward, you force your opponent to try to kill the ball again. He should put away the setup you've given him, but if he leaves it up slightly or skips it in, you may come out smelling like a rose.

Second, when your opponent knows that you not only can chase down some of his best shots, but you're a threat to kill any setups he gives you, this puts greater pressure on him to execute. He realizes that if he's not hitting the ball perfectly, you're going to keep the rally alive and he's not going to win many easy points; in a tough rally, he may be tempted—out of frustration—to take unreasonable risks in hopes of winning the point early. Which is exactly what you want.

As a match progresses, your retrieving ability can begin to take a psychological toll on most opponents, chipping away at their concentration if they begin to dwell on your "gets" and the times they let you off the hook with poor execution. However, your continual saves are unlikely to have much effect if your opponent knows you're not really a threat to keep pressure on him once you've scrambled back into the rally. You can't rest content by simply being a great retriever because, eventually, advanced opponents will make enough of their setups to keep you at bay; they just have to work a little harder for the victory.

Retrieving ability starts with quick anticipation of your opponent's shot, but you can work on the required movements right at home. Clear a 10-foot area (the distance from the middle of the court to a side wall) and actually practice what it means to extend out with your racquet and swing at an imaginary passing shot that's hugging the wall. Work on that unit—the long cross-over step, a stretch, and then the extended arm and a snapping of the wrist—and see how much distance you can cover today . . . and a month from now. This drill stretches your muscles nicely and gives you a feeling of the racquet control that's required. Do the same thing thrusting forward on a diagonal and back on a diagonal.

Contesting every possible shot is crucial in advanced play. Here, a passing shot is almost past the defender for a winner, but he's extending back, with his hand on the floor for support, trying to at least keep the ball in play with a flicking backhand motion.

Then when you're playing, add that crucial psychological factor: a willingness to "go for it," even if you miss. Let yourself be free to just move and hit, striving for the best shot you can manage under the circumstances, whatever your technique. It's tough to be a good retriever without a little of this reckless abandon. Not that you have to leave your feet and dive for the ball, but be ready to at least stretch your body to the limits. (If you want to dive for the ball—and you know how to do it safely—you'll cover more of the court, but save this risk to your body for high competitive levels.)

COVERING SPECIFIC SHOTS

The Straight-in Kill or Pinch Attempt

When moving into your coverage position and reading your opponent's low-zone intentions, mentally concede the putaways inside of 15 feet—but don't let him lengthen his effective kill-shot area much further than that. The service box, in advanced play, should be a diggable, sometimes killable area once you have the ability to thrust forward and stretch out for your opponent's near kills.

If you see the ball heading into the corner as a pinch, be thinking to yourself, "If he makes it, okay; but when he misses, get to the ball." Know the path the ball is going to take if it's left up and move accordingly to kill, repinch, or drive it away from your opponent.

Against the power player, be ready for the unexpected when he tries a straight-in kill (or a splat) from close along the side wall. This shot may catch the side wall but, because of its speed and the way it has been hit, will come spinning off the front wall with heavy English that can force you to react in various directions.

The defender stretches forward to the short line with his racquet extended as he digs up a kill attempt and keeps the rally alive. See how far you can thrust out like this, while in control, and then work to expand this distance. Just 6 or 9 inches will improve your retrieving ability.

The Overhead

Given the opportunity—generally a short ceiling ball—a skilled opponent will try to force you deep with his overhead *drive*, while he then moves into a strong covering position. Few players can consistently apply this pressure by keeping the ball from rebounding off the back wall, but when your opponent poses this threat, be alert. Watch his stroke carefully and be ready to move immediately.

If you have the necessary skill and confidence, break sideways or on a forward diagonal to cut the ball off on the rise (after its first bounce) and then punch it into a front corner. Otherwise, move back toward the corner, ready to take the ball up the ceiling. You're moving quickly and you'll have trouble getting set for a low-zone attempt; plus, your opponent is ready to cover any left-up shot.

Since the target areas are about 10 feet apart, your opponent's stroke and the position of his body can tell you if he's going to try an overhead drive—toward the middle of the front wall—or a kill attempt, which should be a tight pinch. Rarely will you have to fear the overhead kill, one of the game's most difficult shots. You may need to cover this shot from about 26 or 27 feet if your opponent happens to have unusual accuracy, but the ball will nearly always funnel back into the action zone.

The Ceiling Ball

When your opponent goes to the ceiling, stay deep enough to handle three possible options:

1. If the ball has been hit short, play it as it is coming down off its arc from the front court. You should have plenty of room to set up and go for a good offensive shot.

2. If the ball is coming in long, it will rebound high off the back wall, so let it go by as you move back—then come out with the ball, set up solidly, and go low zone.

3. A good ceiling ball will hit no higher than 2 feet up on the back wall (if you were to allow it to go by), so take it about shoulder level and hit either another ceiling or an overhead drive.

Defending Against the "Z" Ball

You've likely learned through experience that even a well-hit "Z" ball is not a shot to fear as it comes out of a front corner toward the opposite side wall. Your basic task is to anticipate the ball's angle as it caroms off this side wall toward the back wall—and then to choose the best place to make contact. Ideally, you'll have room to let the ball drop low as you set up for an offensive opportunity. But if the ball strikes the side wall deep enough, you may be forced to take it to the ceiling before it becomes an irretrievable shot tight against the back wall. Other times you'll sense that you can let the ball strike the floor and kick off the back wall for a setup.

THE CEILING-BALL RALLY

In a ceiling-ball rally, move off toward the middle of the court to give your opponent room to swing, but stay back and wait for her ceiling shot to funnel back deep, even if it's slightly mis-hit.

If you see that your own ceiling shot is going to come in short and give your opponent an offensive opportunity, move into center court and play off the shot that she leaves up.

The Around-the Wall Ball

Your best strategy against the properly hit around-the-wall ball is to cut it off in the air after it caroms off the side wall and is crossing the heart of the action zone. You've been given an offensive opportunity and you want to capitalize by moving into a position to fly-kill for a winner.

A more defensive option is to let the ball bounce and then take it up to the ceiling, just before it reaches the opposite side wall or just after. Also use good discretion if you're going to let this shot carom off the wall, for too often the ball dies quickly and is tough—if not impossible—to dig out.

CUTTING OFF THE AROUND-THE-WALL BALL

When appropriate, the best defense against an around-the-wall ball is to cut the shot off in the air (after it comes off the left side wall), either pinching it into the corner or going for the kill or pass. When the ARWB comes in short of the hitting area shown here, let it bounce and then go for a scoring shot. If it comes in too high or hard, let it carry off the back wall for a setup.

However, with experience in reading this shot along its entire path, you'll know when the ball's been hit too high and you can let it go by, confident that it will carom nicely off the back wall. Similarly, when you see the ball come in too short off the side wall, just let it bounce and then set up for your kill attempt.

Even when you're alone you can practice defending against the around-the-wall ball. For example, stand at about 25 feet and hit the shot into either side wall. Study the ball's path and what it does after coming off the walls. Then start moving into positions where you're comfortable at hitting the ball on the fly as it angles downward (a more difficult skill than it appears). Although you may go an entire match without seeing this shot, make sure you work against it in practice so that you're ready to respond aggressively against the occasional opponent who plays a slow, methodical game and likes to hit one around-the-wall ball after another. Also, at higher playing levels, when an opponent, uses it to "buy time" as he retrieves, you don't want to let him climb easily back into the rally.

The Shot into the Back Wall

When an opponent drives your shot into the *back* wall your coverage will depend upon how well he manages to hit the ball.

● If he drives the ball on an upward angle, it may carry to the ceiling and take a ceiling-ball pattern. You can't cut this shot off before it bounces, but it generally lacks enough force to reach the back wall, so stay deep and prepare to go low zone.

● If he drives the ball straight into the back wall with reasonable velocity, it will rebound directly off the front wall and carry in the air back to around 25 or 30 feet. Instead of cutting it off, let it bounce and come off the back wall as a plum.

● If he barely reaches your shot and takes an off-balance swing, anticipate a weakly hit ball and move forward quickly so you can fly-kill it as it comes off the front wall, somewhere before the short line. Hustle up there, for if you hesitate, the ball will bounce and may force you to quickly retreat and hit from as deep as 35 feet while your opponent moves into a good covering position.

When Your Shot Travels Off the Back Wall to the Front Court

Occasionally you are going to hit the ball so hard and so high that it travels in the air from the front wall to the back wall and then rebounds way forward, offering your opponent a plum in the front court. Where should you position yourself?

Some players like to move right up behind their opponent, trying to distract him into a skip or hoping to somehow dig up his kill attempt. This might work the first time against some opponents, but a smart player knows that his opponent can easily drive the ball past him if he keeps his head. A sounder strategy is to simply position yourself around 22 feet as your opponent is moving up to hit. He should score, but if he leaves the ball up just 12 inches, it will travel back into your hittable area and you may suddenly win the point or gain a side-out with an efficient passing shot.

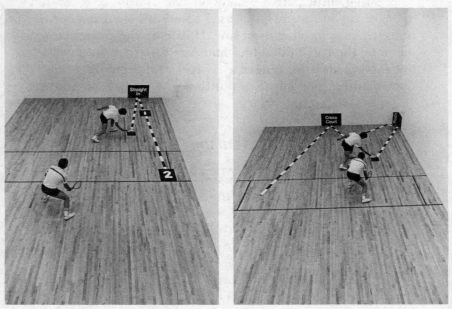

If your offensive shot travels well off the back wall and into the front court *(left)*, take a basic position in center court and at least force your opponent to hit an accurate scoring shot. In the situation here, his best shot is a straight-in kill attempt that, if left up, will still travel down-the-line and extend you to the side of the court.

When you run up behind the hitter *(right)*, trying to rush him or to dig up his straight-in kill attempt, he should adjust his shot selection and either drive the ball cross-court or pinch it away from you.

AVOIDABLE HINDERS

Be assertive in assuming your coverage position, but also be reasonable. Have a respect for your opponent—and the spirit of the game—by giving him room to hit straight-in to the front wall, to go cross-court, and to pinch using the nearest side wall (as shown here). This still leaves you in the best position to reach a high percentage of his shots. A gray area here involves your opponent's hitting lane to the opposite front corner when you're positioned ahead of him. Some people interpret the rule to mean that the hitter must be given clearance to hit this reverse pinch if he chooses. Others feel that if he can go down-the-line and cross-court along with his regular pinch using the left wall, he has enough shot diversification to beat you. This question is still open for debate.

CHAPTER 10

SHOT-SELECTION STRATEGY

Chaotic as this game may seem when you and your opponent are locked in a furious low-zone rally, winning racquetball is built around a systematic approach to shot-selection strategy. I'll agree that your thinking must be as automatic as possible in those quick transitions from covering a shot to hitting, and very often you'll be ad-libbing the best shot you can manage under the circumstances. Yet there's an overall philosophy that can be ingrained in your playing style—a blend of aggressiveness, patience, and flexibility—so that you're attempting the right shots as often as possible. You may mis-execute, but you'll certainly win more points and more matches by having a rhyme and a reason for the shots you are taking.

PLAYING THE PERCENTAGES—
AGGRESSIVELY

An intelligent strategy is built around a number of key concepts.

1. Know Your Game

Evaluate your game through self-critiquing and by having a friend chart several of your matches so that you gain an objective view of your shot-making capabilities. For example: What is your scoring potential from specific areas of the court? How consistently are you hitting your low-zone target areas from both sides of the court—when you're set up and when you're under pressure? How accurate are your pinches into each corner? How precise are your passing shots? Can you keep the ball off the back wall and from mis-angling into the side walls? Do you have a consistent ceiling ball that keeps your opponent pinned deep? Do you have an effective overhead to get out of a long ceiling-ball rally?

Once you've assessed your strokes, you can devise a game plan that is built around the shots you hit best and is adjustable to any opponent's playing style. Know your game and you'll tend to play the percentages, not your whims; instead of trying to out*guess* your opponent, you'll be trying to out*think* him (and outexecute him with sound shot selection).

2. Execute the Basic Shots

In advanced play, you beat your tough opponents with solid shots—not junk shots. Although you're sometimes forced to do whatever you can just to keep the ball in play, rely on the basic shots that are available to you: straight-in kills, pinches, passes, ceiling balls, and the occasional overhead drive. Court coverage and psychological factors will certainly bear on the outcome, but a good match should still come down to the basic question: *Who can execute the right shots when the pressure's on?* You may know the shot to take and you may have position on your opponent, but if there are flaws in your stroke or if you haven't worked on hitting the right target areas, you're going to fight an uphill battle. Skill levels are rising everywhere, at every level of play, and the better players are learning to capitalize on slight errors in execution that give them just the opening they need to take the offensive—from all parts of the court.

3. Kill the Ball When the Opportunity Is There

The overriding emphasis in racquetball today is on hitting with power and going for a winner (kill or pass) at

When two players with similar ability and sound strategy go toe-to-toe, execution will prove decisive (left). Here's a situation where the hitter has an offensive opportunity and she must go for it by hitting straight-in or pinching—knowing that her opponent has good position and is ready to move quickly forward or to the right to cover any left-up shot.

This is a common situation in advanced racquetball, where the player with a particularly strong forehand will swing over and hit that forehand from the left side of center (right). Since the defender is out of position, the hitter's most logical shot is a down-the-wall pass. However, the pinch must also be used in certain situations to keep a balanced attack.

every *reasonable* opportunity. This is a rude awakening for many of the true defensive players, and it's a crucial break-through to make, for when you get the chance, you must go for the shot that will end the rally or draw a weak return from your opponent—before he beats you to the knockout punch. When shooting low into the front wall, you ob-viously risk skipping the ball, but you can't afford to back off by always opting for a "safer" shot. If you simply move the ball around the court, hoping that your opponent will

Although the hitter has the defender off to his right, out of position, he can't logically gamble by going for the straight-in kill on the right half of the front wall *(left)*. He should hit a cross-court kill or pass, or a pinch that carries the ball away from his opponent.

At higher playing levels, you must be willing—and able—to take the offen-sive at the slightest opportunity, even when your opponent has good cen-ter-court coverage ahead of you *(right)*. The hitter here will pinch the ball into the right corner and try to make it die in front of her opponent.

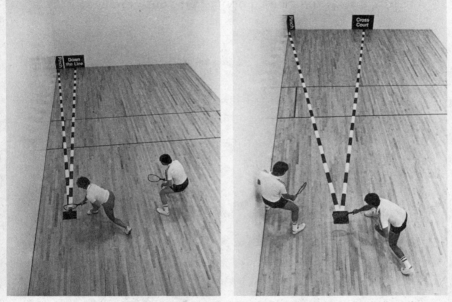

Another attribute of advanced players is their ability to keep the ball on the left side of the court with the backhand—and being offensive with it by killing the ball straight-in, tight pinching it, or taking it back down-the-line *(left)*. This forces the defender to respect the left wall and front court rather than simply lagging deep to the right side of the court in anticipation of a predictable cross-court pass.

Since the hitter now has his opponent positioned off, right against the side wall as he hits his backhand *(right)*, he now wants to be able to pinch the ball away from his opponent or drive it cross-court down the right wall.

When hitting a backhand from deep on the left side, strive for the ultimate goal of having these 3 shots in your arsenal. This offensive diversification will keep your opponent honest, even when he's positioned perfectly in center-court.

skip the ball or give you an absolute plum, you'll be at his mercy far too many times. It's too hard to score 21 points by passing and moving the ball against a player of this quality, because the more you keep the ball in play, the greater the chance that one of your shots will come off the wall as a setup.

I have a friend, a top open player from Wisconsin, who typifies how the game is evolving. He spent several months working on his game in San Diego (where the excellent overall quality of play is strongly influenced by the many touring pros who make their homes there), and he soon recognized an important difference in shot-making philosophy from the one back home. "I've got to make the shot here," he told me. "I can't pass up any of my scoring opportunities." Going against open players in San Diego, he felt an intense pressure to take these shots whenever possible—*and to execute them*, because if he didn't, his opponent would seize the offensive and have the shot-making ability to score or to keep him retrieving.

4. Think Offensively, But Use Your Head

Killing the ball belongs at the forefront of your attack, but there's a lot more to shot selection than simply going for the ultimate winner, whatever the circumstances. As hard and as fast as this game must be played, try to also develop a patience and the good sense to know when to play defensively and when to use one shot to set yourself up for a better shot.

Even the top power players try to think in this manner: *If they don't feel confident about going for the outright winner, they drive the ball; and if they can't pass or move the ball effectively, they go to the ceiling.* Instead of risking an error by forcing an offensive shot, they're content to push their opponent deep and then, through an interchange of ceiling balls, wait for a better opportunity to shoot.

"Playing the percentages" shouldn't be interpreted as a conservative approach to shot-making. To me, it means you want to be thinking offensively, but when you're not in a position to go for a winner, you try to drive your opponent out of position with a solid passing shot that generates a weak return . . . then you go for this higher-percentage kill. And when you feel you're out of your low-zone range, don't count on miracle shots to bail you out of trouble. Instead of gambling by going for spectacular winners that you will almost always skip or leave up, learn to pop the ball to the ceiling and wait out the situation. Your opponent may set you up a lot quicker than you think.

5. Keep Your Opponent Moving

"Hit the ball away from your opponent" is such a fundamental concept that it's easily overlooked in the search for more exotic approaches to strategy. Yet the fact is: when you can force your opponent to hit while he's on the move or stretched out, you greatly reduce his ability to kill the ball. At higher playing levels, many of your opponents will still manage to hit well under pressure. Yet even in the pros, *most kills still come off setups.* Give a good player time to set up and he'll bury the ball, but improve your ball placement and make him hit on the run and he'll give you more shots than you thought were possible. (In a tournament, this can help explain why a player can look like an All-Star in the first round, against an opponent who is continually setting him up, and then get blown out in the second round by an opponent who forces him to cover the entire court under considerable pressure.)

6. Avoid the Feast-or-Famine Approach

Many power players are caught up in a feast-or-famine approach to shot-making, where they try to bomb the ball as hard and as low as they can whenever it comes into their hittable area—even if a reasonable kill-shot opportunity doesn't exist. Win or lose, they keep flailing away until the rally ends with a skip or a kill. By blasting like this with great velocity, they can leave opponents with little reaction time and cause them to be jammed or to miss many shots. However, they also play with virtually no margin for error between their skips and back-wall setups, and they invariably run hot and cold. If they're "feasting," they're hard to stop, but if they're behind, they generally know only one way to turn the momentum around—and that's to somehow become more accurate with their shots (which is difficult to do when they can't seem to keep the ball in their low zone in the first place). Many of these players don't even know that another aspect of strategy exists, and if they do, they often lack the necessary patience and the proper strokes: for example, efficient passing shots that push their opponent deep or to the sides, thereby generating many weak returns.

7. Keep Your Skips Under Control

In a game where you must go for winners at every reasonable opportunity, skips are going to be a fact of life. Don't allow this to inhibit your offensive approach, but work hard to minimize their number so that you make your opponent earn his points. When you're continually hitting the floor by always going for unreasonable kills, realize that your opponent is going to gladly let you dig your own grave. Don't give him easy points; make him earn them.

In going low zone, try to adhere to my "two-bounce" approach, where you avoid continual skips but strive to hit your shots low enough to make them bounce twice before the back wall. Or, think in terms of *pressure plus movement*. When you have good accuracy and you keep the ball off the back wall, your opponent is going to be forced either to cut the ball off or to retreat to deep court quickly, knowing that if the ball gets past him, it's not going to come off the back wall as a setup.

DIVERSIFY YOUR ATTACK

Many players have one good offensive shot from a certain area on the court, and they tend to take that shot consistently and predictably, no matter where their opponent is positioned—especially in pressure situations. These tendencies in your own game will, as we know, give your experienced opponents an important edge by allowing them to move early to where a particular shot tends to locate—thus putting even greater pressure on you to execute. *So stay constantly alert as you play that you're not falling into predictable shot-making patterns.* Work not only on having a variety of offensive shots from both sides of the court, but on keeping a diversification of these shots from the same locations. As an ultimate goal: when you're going low zone, your opponent should be studying your stroke knowing he has to be ready to cover either your down-the-wall kill or pass, the cross-court kill or pass, pinch shots, and perhaps the potential splat winner. If you can have these shots in your arsenal, you'll force him to play you honest in his coverage while delaying his anticipation until the last instant.

Nor can you afford to get so caught up in just hitting the ball that you're oblivious to where your opponent is positioning himself as you set up. For example, when you go to hit a backhand, is he already shading off to the right, anticipating your cross-court pass and challenging you to go down-the-wall? Or, can you sense that he's playing a little too far forward or perhaps lagging too far back? Since it's much easier to see patterns of play from the gallery or on videotape, here are two ways to help your self-awareness. First, have a friend chart one of your matches and note your shot selection with both the forehand and backhand when you go low zone. Are you in a rut, failing to be creative? Or are you constantly making little adjustments that catch your opponent off balance? Second, try to watch one of your matches on videotape, looking for the same patterns in your shot selection and also how your opponent anticipates them.

One practical starting point for shot selection is this rule of thumb: "Pinch the ball when your opponent is behind you, pass when he's ahead of you." Unfortunately, you can't afford to follow this hard-and-fast guideline in more advanced play. If you always try to pinch when he's behind you, he'll move forward to the anticipated path of the ball. And, if you always try to pound the ball past him when he's ahead of you, he'll simply lag, thus narrowing your effective passing lanes.

EXPLOITING YOUR OPPONENT'S WEAKNESSES

Early in the match against an unfamiliar opponent (such as in a tournament or league play), you're going to be probing for weaknesses by applying pressure to both sides of the court. Although your tendency may be to start out by playing defensively, waiting to see what he can do, try to come out aggressively; *throw your best shots at him and test out his skills immediately*. If you're physically and mentally ready to play, his weaker areas may surface quickly when you open up like this.

Early in the first game, find out if your opponent can move quickly to both corners and handle your low-drive and "Z" serves. Mix in some lobs and high "Z's" to see how well he can adjust to a slower pace. If his backhand or forehand corner is a glaring weakness on the serve return, producing numerous skips and left-up shots, keep pouring the ball into this corner and force him to execute. If you try to be an All-American hero by playing to his stronger side, just to show everybody you have diversification, he could easily rip a few winners and change the entire flow of the match.

Once a rally gets under way, your tough opponents will force you to vary your shots because they don't have any real exploitable areas. But when you find a particular weakness, start focusing here and see what your opponent can do under persistent pressure. He may have a strong backhand when he has a chance to set up, but not when he must hit one after another while on the move or stretched out. So don't let him off the hook.

Coping With the One-Stroke Artist

If your opponent has reached an advanced level with a glaring weakness, then very likely he has learned how to effectively compensate for this deficiency while using his strong characteristics to gather enough points to win many matches. Most one-stroke artists like this have a wicked forehand, which normally means a powerful serve, and they're able to run around most shots to their backhand, covering perhaps three-quarters to four-fifths the width of the court with their forehand. The best way to beat a player like this is to attack his backhand weakness, but without getting tunnel vision to this side. Since he's over-playing his backhand as you go to hit, he'll give you obvious scoring opportunities down the open right side of the court—if you can drive the ball forcefully and accurately down this alley. He may give you more setups than you would expect, and if you can now snap an efficient shot to his backhand side, he'll find it hard to run around and save himself with a forehand.

Don't Ignore the Forehand Side

If your opponent has a strong serve, you may fear hitting to what you sense is going to be an equally dangerous forehand. Or, you may be so conditioned to attacking the "weaker" backhand side that you give his forehand more respect than it deserves. So remember: a person may serve very hard and hit the forehand hard—*when he's set up*. But keep that stroke under pressure with good shots, make him stretch over to the right wall, and bring the ball in to that deep corner at different heights, and you may find that his forehand is a lot weaker than you'd realized. (And, of course, some players are simply more efficient with their backhand.) So make sure you're not neglecting the forehand side as the match progresses.

In practice, work on hitting all your shots to both sides of the court so that you're familiar with all the appropriate angles—not only for when you need to exploit a right-hander's vulnerable forehand, but a lefty's ineffective backhand.

ADJUSTING YOUR SHOT SELECTION

Try to go into all of your matches with a flexible game plan, where you've reviewed the shots you want to hit in particular situations, you've anticipated different playing styles, and you've thought through how you'll try to make any necessary adjustments. By taking this approach beforehand, there's far less chance you'll get caught by surprise once play begins and you'll have more confidence in trying different strategies that may help turn the winning momentum your way. I know that I play my best when I go into a match really open for whatever may happen. *I have a definite plan of attack, but I can adjust according to how I'm executing and how my opponent is executing.*

Never underestimate the success you can have against many of your opponents by knowing how and when to throw a new strategy at them. Too many players, I'm afraid, are basically inflexible when they go out to play. They enter the court with tunnel vision, conditioned to play one certain type of game—win or lose—and they're often unable to cope with the opponent who can force them out of that playing style. This is true even at the pro level. So work on all your strokes in order to gain the security to stretch your imagination and try different approaches in shot selection, instead of being scared to make changes for fear they'll lead you to an embarrassing defeat.

Through experience, learn to maintain an overview of how you and your opponent are playing. Keep calculating what shots are working best for you, why certain shots are not working, and how your opponent's positioning and coverage abilities—and tendencies—may dictate a different emphasis in your shot selection. It's easy to get so caught up in the emotions of a match, or to lose your concentration, that you fall into comfortable ruts instead of constantly visualizing subtle changes that might catch your opponent off-balance. So whenever there's a break in the action—a time-out, an equipment change, toweling off a wet spot on the floor—use those moments not just to catch your breath but to think through what is happening in the match and how you might adjust your shot selection.

When your game plan is working, stick with it and just keep pegging out the points. For example, if you came out shooting, and everything is rolling out, continue to be the aggressor. When you lapse into a cautious approach by becoming more selective with your shots as you try to protect your lead—or to gain those last 3 points in the game—that's a different style than the one you've been winning with. Players get caught in this situation all the time and once they lose their momentum, they often are unable to get it back.

Let's say, however, that the match is not going well for and you're falling steadily behind. Obviously you must do some quick and serious thinking. Ask yourself, "Is my game plan sound—but am I just not executing my shots? Or should I be playing my opponent another way?" This determination is a skill acquired through playing experience, but the key issue is that you're open to this analysis during the match and are willing to make the necessary changes when appropriate.

Bringing Off-Speed into the Game

Learn to sense when your aggressiveness in a match is costing you too many points, and it's time to use more discretion in going for the putaway. Start hitting more ceiling balls and concentrate on well-placed passing shots as you try to give your opponent more of a chance to make the first mistake in a rally.

However, if he's hammering you to pieces in a low-zone type of game, you've got to try to take away his hammer. So bring off-speed shots into the game and force him to shift gears as he tries to adjust to a much more deliberate tempo. On the serve, if you haven't been making headway with your low-drives and hard "Z's," start lobbing the ball. Your opponent may not have the temperament or the strokes to play a ceiling-ball game, and he could give you a number of setups as he tries to create some action by taking the ball low. Once a rally is underway, try going to the ceiling more often to keep him from settling back into a low-zone groove. Here, too, you may draw some errors through his impatience or his lack of a consistent ceiling-ball shot.

Basically, *do all you can to keep your opponent from playing his game.* Changing your shot-making strategy may only stall him momentarily—if he can make the necessary adjustments—but this may be long enough to help you work your way back into the match.

Taking the Offensive

When you decide that you're falling behind by playing too defensively, it's time to open up your offense and take some chances in your shot selection. For example, if you've been going back to the ceiling when you've had some scoring chances, or if you're passing the ball instead of putting it down, get yourself into a more aggressive frame of mind. Go for the kill at the slightest opening; jump on that scoring opportunity before your opponent gets his chance.

Again, this contrast in game styles may catch your opponent off-guard and unable to adjust quickly, allowing you to cut away at his lead. But for that to happen, you can't afford to let your eagerness to create action lead to unreasonable kill attempts that simply help feed your opponent's momentum.

Responding to Your Opponent's Adjustments

While you're trying to draw conclusions as you play, hoping to make the most sensible adjustments, a tough opponent will be doing the same and forcing you to respond. If your power game was working well as you won the first game, you can expect this opponent to come out in the second game and force you to handle a series of different off-speed serves as he tries to prevent you from playing your game. Here's where you must have confidence in your control game and the patience to go back up to the ceiling when the offensive opportunity isn't there, but also the ability to take the ball down low when you see the slightest opening.

CHAPTER 11

IMPROVING YOUR GAME

If you've been relying on playing experience to lift your game another notch, you may be thinking, "I'm playing twice a week, but I'm not improving, so I'll add a third day." Unfortunately, natural athletic ability and years of experience can take you only so far in this game. When you're seeking long-term improvement and striving for an all-round game, you must set aside time each week to actually work on your stroking technique and all of your shots—free of the pressure and the shortcomings of trying to win a match. Even if it's only a 30-minute session, or an extra 10 minutes before you play, get by yourself or with a friend and really *practice* with a purpose in mind. At higher playing levels, this time is vital not only to maintain your current playing level, but to incorporate new shots into your game.

This chapter will help you organize your practice time, by mixing workout sessions with practice matches, so that you have fun as you make some worthwhile advances. I'll also discuss ways you can improve your play without even hitting the ball, through better conditioning. (However you practice, loosen up properly beforehand, such as by using the stretching exercises shown later in this chapter in the conditioning section. More pulled muscles result from an incomplete warm-up than from any other cause.)

PRACTICING ALONE

Like a golfer at a driving range, it's important that you know how to practice by yourself, whether it's a planned session or an unexpected 5 minutes when your playing partner is late arriving. Use this time for concentrating on stroking technique, to improve your power and control, and to test different shots—without the distractions of another player. The following ten drills will give you all your important shots (except for the service return) a realistic workout, using the walls as a perfect backboard.

1.   As a confidence-builder and to work on your timing, stand at about 25 feet, drop the ball, and hit it off the bounce as low as you can into the front wall. Get used to hitting one winner after another, striving for an early setup, a whipping action as you stroke the ball, and solid racquet contact. Practice forehands like this for about ten hits, then move back a couple of feet. Keep moving back until you're next to the back wall—then switch to your backhand and start the process all over again.

2.   For a better game-type situation, hit the ball easily to yourself off the front wall so it comes back into your power-hitting zone. Focus on your stroking motion and strive to put the ball away, but avoid constant skips and try to keep your misses low enough so they bounce twice before the back wall. Hit from both sides of the court and work your way back to 38 feet. Just for fun, save your ball cans and line them up along the front wall. You'll likely discover that it takes much longer than imagined to actually knock one over.

3.   Practice rallying up and down each side wall, work-

ing on just one stroke at a time, but continually readjusting your position and hitting a variety of shots: straight-in kills, down-the-line passes, ceilings, and balls off the back wall. This is an adjustable, ad-lib type of drill—just like in a real match—and your goal is to kill the ball at every opportunity, while trying to keep it off the side wall. If the ball bounces two or three times before it reaches you, still hit it back to the front wall to keep a continuous rally going. When you're forced to the middle of the court, slide over quickly and try to drive the ball down the wall with the same stroke.

4.   Now shift from straight-in kills and passes to corner pinch shots. Starting from about 25 feet and moving your way back, practice pinching low and hard so the ball bounces twice before reaching the opposite side wall or the front red line. One way to start this drill is to drive the ball off the front wall into the side wall so that it comes back to you in the center-court area (thus simulating a typical rally situation). For variety, you can also practice going down-the-wall or cross-court against balls coming out of the front corner.

5.   To work on your reaction-type shots, stand at about 25 feet and start a low-zone rally by hitting the ball with good pace to the front wall. Be aggressive and cut off as many shots as you can that come through your area at waist height or lower. Go for the putaway (straight-in or as a pinch), but don't worry if you skip the shot or leave it up 6 feet. The object is to hone your center-court play by becoming a little more daring while working on your stroking technique from different footwork positions.

6.   Now progress and work on shots that come off the back wall. Practice moving back far enough with the ball so that as it rebounds you can move forward and hit an offensive shot.

7.   Hit ceiling balls to yourself up and down both walls and try to see how long you can keep a ceiling-ball rally going. If that shot is long, short, or off the side wall, take it

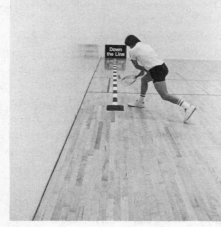

This player is practicing by himself, just dropping the ball (or setting himself up) to start a rally along the left wall, and then striving to keep his backhand shots off the wall. Learn to keep this rally going as long as possible by moving laterally in about a 10-foot area, using shuffle steps and cross-over steps, while hitting from different stances.

down into your low zone, just as you would in a match. Mix in some overhead drives against the short ceiling to diversify your offensive attack. Also, practice hitting your ceilings cross-court so you're comfortable directing the ball to the backhand corner against a right-hander and a left-hander.

8. In practicing your serve, have at least four or five balls available to save time. Then focus on a number of key elements: your front-wall targets, your two-step motion into the ball, your stroke, the accuracy of your serves and your relocation.

9. Unless there's a ball machine for rent at your club, you can't really practice hitting your service return by yourself—but you can emulate the desired movements. Assume your normal waiting position, then angle a ball into either

corner and follow it over by taking your cross-over step and a long stretch. Practice hitting the ball offensively and defensively in this drill.

10.   Now you're ready for a one-person rally covering your entire hittable area. Start the rally and just keep it going with all the shots in your arsenal, taking the appropriate shot—in most situations—but going for the putaway at every opportunity. You've already worked on kills off easy setups; now practice being offensive when you're under pressure, on the move, and in uncomfortable hitting positions. At times, shoot the ball no matter how impossible the kill may seem, just to get a feel for those shots that you will some day want to incorporate into your attack. Since many of your low-zone shots will be catching a side wall as you hustle from one side of the court to the other, you'll have a chance to cover the different-angled shots that will challenge you in a match.

To help make these solitary practice sessions more enjoyable—while sharpening your concentration—use your imagination to simulate game situations. Become a kid again, fantasizing yourself in the finals of a big tournament. For example, it's 10–all in the tiebreaker and you're in a ceiling-ball rally. The pressure is intense. You're hitting for both players and you see your opponent's ceiling coming in short. So you're thinking, "I'm going for the flat rollout. I need this point to win the championship." Can you now execute?

PRACTICING WITH A FRIEND

Treasure the person who wants to spend time practicing his game without a need to rush right into a competitive match, for he (or she) is going to help you improve immensely. Here are realistic practice drills the two of you can incorporate into a workout, with mutual benefits.

1. Adapt some of the individual drills given earlier by simply dividing the court, with one person hitting forehands to the other person's backhand. One example would be to stand on opposite sides at about 35 feet and work on deep cross-court passing shots. This sounds easy, but you both may be humbled by how short some of these rallies are.

2. Start a ceiling-ball rally and play it out to a conclusion, but remember: your basic goals are to focus on your stroking technique, read your opponent's ceiling (seeing how early and accurately you can decide your intentions as the ball approaches), and breaking up the rally with a low-zone shot. Also, when you see that your friend is going low, practice studying his stroke and moving into proper coverage position.

3. Move up to around 23 or 24 feet and start a low-zone "reflex" drill, with both of you trying to cut the ball off and put it away. This is a difficult drill to sustain beyond two or three hits, but it still gives you experience reacting quickly to a ball off the front wall and using adaptable form (another typical situation that is going to come up many times in a match).

4. Put a few cans along the front wall and hit easy setups to each other off the front wall. See how many shots it takes to knock a can over, and who can do it first. The loser buys the next can of balls.

5. Another challenging drill is to rally up and down a side wall, with both players going for straight-in kills and down-the-line passes. (If the ball comes back too high, play it off the back wall.) This can be a humbling experience if you think it's easy to keep the ball off the side wall for more than six or seven hits. But it's also an excellent way to groove into that sequence of watching your opponent's stroke until impact, then turning to the front wall and reacting.

6. To end a workout, have one player hit five serves while the other hits five returns, then alternate. Play each

This is an excellent drill for working on a down-the-line backhand, with both players trying to keep the ball going up and down the left side. Here, the player up front is practicing holding his position and cutting the ball off when appropriate, and he'll interchange positions with his partner when he's driven deep.

Players take their forehands for granted and think it's easy to rally up and down the right wall. Try this drill with a friend and you'll realize that it's harder than it looks.

rally to the end if you want, but don't keep score, since you want to avoid the ego involvement that comes with worrying about who's "winning" the most points. Instead, *feel free about experimenting with something new or concentrating on a particular problem area.* For example, as the returner you might want to see just how many serves you can hit back down the line for winners. You may skip a few balls and leave a lot up, but that's no big deal to either player, because you're working on a more offensive approach—and your opponent is focusing on aspects of his serve.

PLAYING PRACTICE MATCHES

When you're involved in organized competition such as tournaments, leagues, and challenge ladders, your other matches should take two approaches.

First, you'll want to schedule matches where you're going all-out to win against a strong opponent—hitting your best shots, getting into long rallies, and staying in touch with playing the pressure points. Second, and more important, arrange matches where you're concentrating on specific areas of the game and the final result is not really a concern. (To me, an ideal workout would include several practice games with this philosophy and several games to 11 or 15 where you try to play with tournament intensity.)

Whatever your competitive nature, when it comes to making long-term gains, *reward yourself for working on improvement, not for how many practice matches you win.* As you try to improve your stroking technique or add a new shot, you may feel a little awkward at times and you usually must work through a stage where your efficiency goes down when you play. Don't worry; the polish will come through *patience and persistence.* But if winning is an overriding priority every time you go out to play, then these values get

short-circuited, for it's human nature to scrub what is uncomfortable, unfamiliar, or unproductive and—under pressure—to revert to the same old way of playing.

So, you must have practice matches where you can experiment freely with your game, exploring new areas and
trying out a particular shot you've been afraid to use in
your competitive matches, for fear of losing an important
point or a side-out. Take this opportunity to break away
from your comfortable shot-selection patterns and work on
the shots you'll eventually need to beat your tough opponents. For example:

● If you always hit cross-court passes with your backhand, try hitting a few down-the-line. If you can't do it
without a skip or a shot that travels around the walls and
comes off as a plum, go to work on your technique in practice sessions.

● Look for opportunities to hit a reverse pinch.

● Try to cut more balls off.

● Hit some overhead drives off the short ceiling ball,
instead of always taking it back to the ceiling.

● Strive for more power on your low-drive serve by
covering a longer distance with your two-step motion and
getting lower with your body as you swing.

● When you see your opponent edging too far forward as you move to set up for a forehand, practice hitting
the wide-angled pass to get the ball around him.

In arranging practice matches, test your game by opening yourself up to stiffer competition. Better players will
challenge you to execute more efficiently, to cover more of
the court, and to expand your shot-selection strategy. You
may get blown out, but view the match as an opportunity
to see what progress you're making and where improvements have to be made.

Meanwhile, when you find yourself playing a weaker
opponent—your boss, let's say—use this time as a way to

work on basics. Take some pace off the ball, avoid your kill attempts, and just concentrate on moving the ball around the court with solid passing shots (not dinks) so the two of you can get into decent rallies. Learning to control the ball like this is much harder than you think if you're basically a power player, but it will pay dividends on those days when your kill-shot timing is off and you have to diversify your attack.

ADDING NEW SHOTS TO YOUR GAME

The shots in this book are all valuable in certain situations as you try to gain higher playing levels and you come up against different types of opponents. If you haven't learned to hit all of these shots, or if you realize that you're avoiding certain ones under pressure, then you're limiting your shot-selection potential and the progress you can make in this game. Here are some steps to follow as you work on a shot that will make you a better player up the road.

1. Go on a court by yourself, bounce the ball, and just hit the shot over and over again, learning your target area and the angles involved from a particular location. If it's a reverse pinch, for example, concentrate on where you must hit the opposite side wall to make it work, and study the ramifications of a shot that is hit too high or at the wrong angle. When you miss, notice where you should reposition yourself according to the ball's path and where your opponent is likely going to hit.

2. Have the ball come to you off the front wall, then practice hitting this new shot from different areas on the court. Focus on where the ball travels in relation to where it contacts the front wall, and become familiar with the patterns involved.

3. Start looking for opportunities to hit the shot in practice matches; open up your horizons and don't be afraid to change comfortable but limiting shot-selection habits. However, be careful not to overuse the shot, where you're disrupting the flow of the match and taking the fun out of it for your opponent by constantly skipping the ball or hitting it wildly around the walls.

4. As you begin controlling this shot and gain more confidence, gradually incorporate it into your competitive matches, while learning its virtues and limitations.

5. Always have in mind a specific shot to work on when you go to the club, in case you find yourself with an extra 5 minutes on an empty court. If it's a wide-angled cross-court pass, you can hit a quick twenty-five or thirty shots into the front wall, trying to angle the ball so it strikes the side wall just behind the service box and takes two bounces before the back wall.

6. Work hard but be patient, for it will take time to have this new shot become a comfortable, reflexive, and reliable part of your game. This is exactly how the pros put together a solid game.

WORKING ON YOUR STROKING TECHNIQUE

After reading this book, you may realize that your strokes need a major overhaul—or just some small refinements—to give you more power, control, and consistency. Undoing "muscle-memory" patterns in a swing and making the desired changes is a long process, but certainly worth the time and effort you invest.

Basically, try to incorporate the fundamental checkpoints we've shown in the photographs, but adapt them to your own naturalness. By evaluating your swing in several ways (see below) and just practicing the desired motion on an empty court, you can begin to sense what you want to be doing and mistakes to avoid. Basic flaws may persist, limiting the ultimate effectiveness of a particular stroke, but don't let overall technique inhibit you from broadening your shot selection. If you have a grooved stroking motion on the forehand side—good, bad, or indifferent—you can add almost any shot to your arsenal by using the stroke you have. Simply begin with practice sessions where you hit the ball hundreds of times into the appropriate front- or side-wall target areas, then build from there, trying to refine your stroking technique the best you can.

Have you actually determined your exact low-drive target areas on the front wall? As shown here, have a friend apply small removable stickers to indicate where your serves make contact, while you study the ball's path into the back corner. I think you'll be amazed at how small your target area must be in order to hit effective serves, and how the slightest error in missing this target is magnified in the back court.

EVALUATING YOUR GAME

To go that extra length in improving your game—by uncovering crucial shortcomings in your strokes and court coverage that are choking your progress—seek out the objective feedback offered by a number of outside sources: videotape, a friend who can watch you play, a qualified teaching pro, and even a mirror.

Videotape

Try to have a friend videotape one of your matches and you'll be amazed at what you can learn when you see yourself in action, humbling as that might be to your ego. Videotaping is the most valuable self-teaching device I know, for it allows you to see for yourself just how well you are actually moving to the ball, stroking the ball, and covering your opponent's shots. There may be a big gap between the perception you have of yourself as a racquetball player and how you actually look on the television screen, but that's of great value. I know that it motivates me to go out and work on my game with a fresh and objective perspective.

A knowledgeable player can see the more blatant flaws in your stroke with his naked eye, and point these out to you, but very often it may take videotape to actually convince you just how late you're setting up for your shots, even when there's ample time. Or, when you see your swing in slow motion, you may realize that your follow-through is weak and incomplete, or that your legs are too stiff and not involved in the total swing. Equally important are the discoveries you make about your court coverage—bad habits you may have fallen into unconsciously, deficiencies in your movement to the ball, inefficient relocation after your serve, and so on.

Once you've identified these weaker areas of play, you can go to work on them in practice, then make another tape in 3 or 4 weeks to see for yourself if you're making the desired improvements.

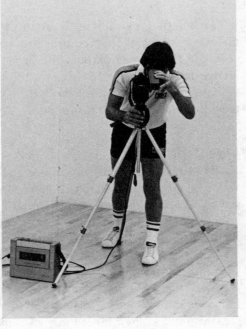

A video-cassette unit is an invaluable tool for recording your stroking technique on a practice court, and to analyze your strategy and positioning under match-play conditions (providing the cameraman films from the gallery, or through a glass wall).

Check around your club for access to videotaping equipment, and share expenses with a playing partner or two; for $15 to $20 you can buy a six-hour tape and use it over and over again, filming each other as you play and studying the results at home.

Other Methods of Evaluation

If videotape isn't practical, try having a friend film all your strokes inside a court with a Super-8 camera, using high-speed film. Or, he can use a 35mm camera. Hit a ball to yourself and have him snap a picture as you're setting up, as you're contacting the ball, and as you follow through. Then you can study key checkpoints right on the contact sheets (using a photographic magnifying glass) without having to make prints.

● Throughout the book I've pointed out many ways a friend can help you improve by evaluating your game from the gallery. If he has a good eye for racquetball technique, he can study your swing as you play a match, using the guidelines and checkpoints you've given him. He can't accurately determine what is happening in the hitting zone, since this action is occurring too fast, but he can give you feedback on what you're doing before and after. He can also notice just how effectively you're covering your opponent's shots.

● When practicing by yourself on the court, it's crucial that you have an accurate image of what you should look like—and what you should be striving for—as you swing. To facilitate this, study your strokes against a mirror, comparing yourself with the photographs in this book and trying to duplicate the key fundamentals. Check your

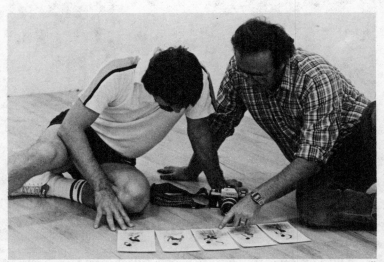

When playing or practicing, you may think you swing a certain way—until you actually see yourself on videotape, or in still photographs. Try to have a friend shoot a roll of black-and-white film as you hit your various shots, and then either look at the contact sheet or some small prints so that you can check your stroking technique against the desired fundamentals.

stroke at different stages by stopping and seeing how you look in the mirror. Get a feel for being in that position, and notice the relationship between your body movement and your racquet position at that stage of the swing. Then go through the stroke in slow motion and, as you watch the different movements happening, concentrate on those sensations. Remember that in the end, when you're on the court hitting, *you have to teach yourself how to play this game right*.

Yet another way to see if you're addressing the correct fundamentals is to check yourself against a mirror.

CONDITIONING

The key question here is: Toward the end of a close match, are you fatiguing to the point where your shot efficiency, concentration, and aggressiveness begin to suffer (not to mention your enjoyment of the game)? If so, then extra conditioning efforts will certainly pay off—not just in a tiebreaker, but throughout the match.

Get into better shape (while also working on your flexibility and stretchability) and you'll find yourself covering more of the court with greater confidence and aggressiveness. I know that *when I'm in top condition, I get more out of my ability*: I can reach the ball quicker, which gives me slightly more time to execute, and I get a little lower with my body as I hit. Meanwhile, I'm a more intense competitor because I know I can play for two hours or more without having to pace myself from rally to rally; if the match is on the line and I have to tap a reserve, I know it's going to be there.

Conversely, when I don't have my stamina, I'm afraid to really push myself by getting into long rallies, because I'm not sure my body can handle the demands and I know it's all going to catch up to me later in the match. So I tend to only play hard in spurts, trying to conserve my energy, and taking more low-percentage kills instead of just grinding it out and trying to win with reasonable fundamental shots.

Basically, I concentrate on three areas in my conditioning: running, stretching and flexibility, and weight training.

Running

I feel that running is the best conditioning exercise for a game like this, where getting to the ball—right down to the last point—is so fundamentally important. As much as I play, I still need to run about 5 miles a day just to maintain my endurance on the pro circuit, while adding short-wind sprints (20 to 30 yards each) for greater quickness and strength in covering the court.

My favorite drill for working on the whole package—agility, leg strength, lateral mobility, and quick starts—is one you can do on a court, on a grassy surface, or at the beach. Have a racquet in your hand and pretend that you're covering the back 20-by-20 area of the court. Dig hard in all directions, seeing how much ground you can cover with a cross-over step and a long stretch, then take a practice swing and move to cover your opponent's shot. Push yourself for 30 seconds and you'll be exhausted.

Stretching

Five minutes of stretching exercises on a daily basis, or at least before your practice sessions and all matches, is an important habit in advanced racquetball.

First of all, when you're properly stretched out, you minimize the chances of muscle pulls and strains; you can play hard with little fear of injury.

Second, working out the stiffness beforehand tends to calm nerves going into a pressure match; psychologically, you know you're ready to get into the flow of action on the first point.

Third, a regular routine of stretching will help counter a natural loss of flexibility as you grow older. When your movement is limited by a lack of stretchability and agility, you can still play a strong game, but you put greater pressure on your shot-making ability to compensate. (In fact, conditioning itself may not be a problem, but your progress could be limited by a stiff body that limits your mobility. Here's where a flexibility class could be of great help, by making your body ready and willing to move and bend to retrieve more shots.)

Weight Training

Playing matches and running give my legs the workout they need, but I've found that I need a regular program of light weight training—not to bulk up, but to maintain strength and durability in my arms, shoulders, and upper body. Working with dumbbell weights provides greater flexibility and power for taking my racquet high on the backswing and whipping it through the stroking motion

STRETCHING EXERCISES

Incorporate these five stretching exercises into your preparation for practice or a match and you'll help your body respond safely—and with greater effectiveness—to the demands of the game.

Leaning or pushing against the wall like this will stretch the calf. You'll actually feel the tightness leaving as you hold the stretch for at least 15 seconds. Then switch legs, putting a little pressure behind the opposite knee. Also do the same exercise with each knee bent to stretch the Achilles tendon and the soleus muscle.

The knee-to-chest stretch will loosen the hamstring muscle. Lie on the floor, bring one knee up toward your chest, then grab the leg with your hands and pull. Keep a constant pressure and you'll be able to get that knee closer and closer to your chest as the blood begins to flow and the muscles loosen. Half a minute or a minute should do one leg, then repeat the drill with the other.

From the same on-the-floor position, point your foot toward the ceiling to stretch the hamstring. Extend the leg and put a little pressure on the back of the thigh. It won't take long, but it'll do a lot of good.

Assume a sitting position on the floor, with your legs pointed out at 45° angles. You're going to touch your nose to your knees (or at least try), bending from the waist and pulling with your arms. If you've done the first three exercises properly, that will help. I suggest you use a constant, 10 to 15 second stretch.

This may not be the most flattering picture ever taken of me, but it's a good exercise. Just lie back and lift your legs back over your head. Try to touch the floor above your head with your toes. Feel your lower back begin to loosen. When you want to rip a powerful backhand, you'll be glad you did this exercise.

with good velocity. Also, when I'm leaning out or stretched out to hit, I have the strength to come through forcefully with a snapping motion.

If there's a weight program at your club, take advantage of it by doing some light lifting about three times a week, before you to out to play. There are also several excellent weight-training machines on the market that can help increase your strength and flexibility.

If your club is minimally equipped with weight-training equipment, just a pair of light dumbbells can be used to work on strength and flexibility in your upper body. Here are several of the exercises I find helpful.

From a basic starting position, take your elbows to a position higher than your shoulders. This is similar to a power setup on your forehand, especially if you were to replace the right weight with a racquet.

This is a similar drill, except that you're taking the weight above your head with the arm extended.

Now hold the weights at your side and take them laterally up your side to above your head.

Starting with two weights held straight out ahead of you, pull them back and then crisscross your arms. I've found that this exercise helps develop strength for pulling the ball down from chest height and going for an aggressive shot.

Conditioning While on the Court

If you intend to stay in top playing shape without an outside regimen, here are some ways you can increase your endurance on the court:

● Find opponents who will give you a tough, competitive match that forces you to work hard. One example would be the hard-nosed retriever, who prolongs many rallies with his "gets."

● Sometimes play with a slow ball, to generate more rallies and to help sustain longer rallies.

● Play the extra game when nobody comes to claim your court or if you find an empty court down the hall.

● Work on practice drills that force you to move continuously. One example: rally up and down one wall (alone or with a friend), trying to keep the action going as long as possible.